T0147166

FACE TO FACE
WITH SPIRIT

FACE TO FACE WITH SPIRIT

An Architect's Journey of Discovery

ESİ ÇAKMAKÇIOĞLU

BALBOA.
PRESS

A DIVISION OF HAY HOUSE

Copyright © 2016 Esi Cakmakcioglu.

All rights reserved. No part of this book may be used or reproduced by
any means, graphic, electronic, or mechanical, including photocopying,
recording, taping or by any information storage retrieval system
without the written permission of the author except in the case of
brief quotations embodied in critical articles and reviews.

Balboa Press books may be ordered through booksellers or by contacting:

Balboa Press
A Division of Hay House
1663 Liberty Drive
Bloomington, IN 47403
www.balboapress.com
1 (877) 407-4847

Because of the dynamic nature of the Internet, any web addresses or
links contained in this book may have changed since publication and
may no longer be valid. The views expressed in this work are solely those
of the author and do not necessarily reflect the views of the publisher,
and the publisher hereby disclaims any responsibility for them.

The author of this book does not dispense medical advice or prescribe the use
of any technique as a form of treatment for physical, emotional, or medical
problems without the advice of a physician, either directly or indirectly. The
intent of the author is only to offer information of a general nature to help
you in your quest for emotional and spiritual well-being. In the event you use
any of the information in this book for yourself, which is your constitutional
right, the author and the publisher assume no responsibility for your actions.

Cover Image by Isik Konuk
Artwork by Ufuk Boy, 2015 "Kapanis 1- iron plates
and wood, 132cm x 33cm x 32 cm"

Print information available on the last page.

ISBN: 978-1-5043-5677-0 (sc)
ISBN: 978-1-5043-5679-4 (hc)
ISBN: 978-1-5043-5678-7 (e)

Library of Congress Control Number: 2016908448

Balboa Press rev. date: 08/18/2016

To My Father

The book is a journey of Esi's discovery of her own spiritual ability, which she has interwoven with experiences of her home and professional life. Esi tells how she developed her mediumship and her gift of drawing spirit, and also of healing. She has shown through her many letters of confirmation of evidence and healing that our loved ones do not die.

Face to Face with Spirit will encourage not only the spiritual novice, but those who are experienced mediums and healers.

Terry Tasker- Medium, Healer and Tutor

Face to Face with Spirit is a fascinating account of Esi's self-discovery through a very personal journey, linking architecture and urban design work built in many different parts of the world to her various gifts that span Spirit drawings, mediumship, healing and clinical hypnotherapy.

I was first introduced to Esi's architectural and urban design work some thirty-five years ago and I have always been impressed with her unique and creative design approaches.

I have also closely followed Esi's self-discovery of her other journeys that led her to the complexities of our inner worlds, endorsed by so many participants, evident in the Spirit drawings that reveal so many unusual stories.

This is an exciting and captivating book, beautifully written, and is sure to appeal to wide-ranging audiences. The book illustrates how we can experience many dimensions of our own worlds, through our own exciting self-discovery.

Dr. Georgia Watson- An Urbanist and Urban Designer

CONTENTS

TABLE OF ILLUSTRATIONS

PREFACE

As the plane took off, I was sitting next to my partner, trying to ignore the pain coming from my toe, which I had broken only hours before leaving Hong Kong for the last time. When we landed in London, my life would change completely.

We would say goodbye and set off in different directions, never to meet again. The exciting architectural projects in hot and humid countries, the flying to different exotic places for both work and holidays, and all the travelling to and from Europe would be left behind.

I didn't want to live in the Far East any more. I missed the European lifestyle, but where could I call home? I had no idea! Could I settle in my flat in London or would it be in Istanbul? I had enjoyed such an adventurous life and experienced so many temporary homes. Until then, fixed plans for more than a month in advance were not a feature of my life; but, no matter where I went, many opportunities for work were given to me. Looking at my life, I seemed to have travelled everywhere but I never belonged anywhere!

Now was the time to settle in to a job and a home, and I knew I had to put a plan in place. What I did not know was that Life had different plans for me!

It was to be the beginning of a journey unlike any other!

ACKNOWLEDGEMENTS

I thank my parents, now in Spirit, for bringing me into life and teaching me to have a curious, creative and independent mind, and for their continuing love and support in my spiritual development.

I owe my gratitude to Kayhan Yildizoglu for introducing me to the Spirit and opening the door into a world of wonder and wisdom.

I feel extremely privileged to be able to pass on the messages from Ibn'i Sina/Avicenna, my guides and my artists, which will continue to enlighten those still on earth.

I am indebted to Jean Reich and Helen Yesugey for their initial 'corrections' of my English when I began putting my very first words to paper while fighting the fears that I am not a writer.

I trusted my guides to lead me to an editor with an open mind, an insight into human psychology, and also the sensitivity to keep the manuscript in my 'voice'. It was a challenging task to achieve but Anthony Sarankin, who is my editor, not only did that but helped me along the way with his constructive criticism and encouragement. Thank you, Anthony.

I feel privileged to be invited to serve in the Spiritualist Churches and centres where those in mourning, in pain or simply curious can visit and seek answers. I am honoured to have had the opportunity to communicate with their loved ones as well as those who trusted me to help them in their journeys. I especially owe a great debt to those who gave me their consent to share their stories with you. These are all true stories, and I use them with permission; even so, in some cases, at the request of the people concerned, I have used only initials or anonymised their names, to keep their identity private.

To all, with my deepest gratitude.

INTRODUCTION

Not long ago, I was presented with a plaque by the Istanbul Metropolitan Branch of the Chamber of Architects to mark my fortieth year as an architect. Yet, almost all of this span of my working life as an architect and urban designer was spent outside Turkey, covering projects in twelve countries: United Kingdom, Turkey, Germany, Saudi Arabia, Kazakhstan, Uzbekistan, Northern Cyprus, Brunei (Borneo), Hong Kong, Myanmar (formerly Burma), China and the Philippines. I have always considered myself lucky and privileged in my professional life.

I've had a busy and adventurous life; my journey has taken me to many places and through many experiences, including the exploration of my emotional past, and a major cancer operation. As with all life journeys, some elements were consciously planned, some not. What wasn't included in my plans was being introduced to Spirit —but that is what happened!

I was first introduced to Spirit in 1987. Although this completely unexpected experience did cause me to question our 'reality', it came at a time when my life was too busy for any serious further involvement or consideration. It took another thirteen years until the doors into this magical world swung fully open to me.

I was brought up in a family of scientists. My father's fields were Mathematics and Astronomy, my mother's Chemistry and Physics. As children, one of our 'playgrounds' was my mother's laboratory at the college. I do believe that my exposure to this scientific environment gave me an enquiring and curious mind.

Like any other child I was curious about the universe and life on earth. Why are we here on earth? Why was I born to be the child I was? What about my friends, my family, all these people on earth? What happens when we die? I was full of questions. Did I, however, ever think I would one day be working with the Spirit and that I would be given answers to my questions and even more? The answer would have been 'No' until the year 2000.

On my return from the Far East in 1999, I set about re-establishing myself in the UK—starting yet another home, and resuming a career as an architect and urban designer. All the while, I made regular trips to Istanbul to care for my frail mother. Throughout this time, however, I was also walking another path, which led to a completely new world full of wisdom and wonders.

The spiritual world that opened in front of me showed me that there really is no death. We are all spirit, dressed temporarily in physical bodies, and 'dying' is simply the shedding of these physical bodies to return to the energy world that we come from.

I now consider myself privileged in that I am able to communicate with the Spirit so that I can help people in mourning and provide them with evidence that life is eternal. This I do both by communicating with their loved ones and sketching the portraits of those in spirit whom they thought were lost forever.

I had no expectations in terms of what all my life experiences were leading me to, so I was not only pleasantly surprised, but grateful, to realise that I was now seeing 'life on earth' in a completely new context — a framework that explains why we are here and how our lives are shaped from birth to death by the choices we make along the way. More importantly, it is this understanding that not only empowers us but also brings meaning to our lives.

I hope the stories I relate and the portrait drawings I have included will lead you to the same conclusions I came to. That is, that consciousness doesn't reside in our brains but belongs to spirit.

On a recent visit to the Spiritual Association of Great Britain (SAGB) in London, one of its respected mediums, Terry Tasker, gave me a message from my late father. This is what it said:

Dare to be a Daniel[1]
Dare to stand alone

---

[1] Referring to the story of Daniel in the Old Testament, who had been pressurised to change his beliefs by the Pagan king and thrown into the lion's den when he refused to comply.

Dare to have a truth
Dare to make it known

I have never considered writing to be one of my gifts! I never kept a diary until I was introduced to the Spirit, but fascinated by this new world in which I found myself, I began to keep notes. This proved far-sighted, because my scribblings have enabled me to recall the details of the most exciting journey of my life.

Encouraged by my father's message, I started to write. Then I found that I had a dilemma; I knew what it was that I had to make known and, further, that to be a true account it could be based only on my own experiences and what I have witnessed along the way. That is how I decided to tell my truth through my journey, in the hope that it may be a starting point for your own.

MEETING IBN'I SINA (AVICENNA)

1- Ibn'i Sina (Avicenna) 980-1037 (Drawn 5.1.2005)

My first introduction to the Spirit was through a friend's father, Kayhan, who has now become a dear friend in his own right. He is an actor, and genuinely the most eccentric person I have ever met. At the time, he lived in Istanbul. I did not know anyone who had been communicating with the Spirit until I met him.

In July 1987, I was visiting my mother in Istanbul when I was invited to sit at two Spirit communication seances with him. The invitation came from his daughter and her husband, whom I had known since I was a young girl. We had several communicators. Each had a different way of expressing themselves, some using old words, redundant now, as is to be expected when talking to an elderly relative. The most striking for me was the communication with Ibn'i Sina whose European name is Avicenna[2].

---

[2] 980- 1037 Scholar, Poet. Born in a large village in Kharmaithan, near Bukhara and died in June or July in Hamadran, aged 58. Author of *The Canon of Medicine*—his chief medical work—and *Shifa*—book of philosophy— among many others in metaphysics, psychology, logic, and religion, which were taught in medical schools throughout Europe.

Five years before, I'd had an operation for cancer. For this reason, the questions I raised were centred on the reasons for my illness, and what his recommendations might be. His replies were all related to 'energy' and 'essence' and 'spiritual power'. It was rather puzzling for me at the time, but writing furiously, I took notes. It was only years later that I appreciated his advice.

His first words were "life cannot be shortened or extended", and that "I did not need to be scared of dying". Below is a transcript of our conversation (The words in parenthesis are the questions relating to me, put to him by the members of the seance group):

"You are all spiritually cleansing."

(Someone said to her that her 'sun light' is blocked. Is it true?)

"What are you talking about? All is from the divine power. She is going into a new chapter in her life. She is a very giving person. She does not save her energy and that makes her depleted."

(How can she save that energy?)

"She should know her 'essence'."

(What do you mean by 'essence'?)

"She is a spiritually strong person but she is not putting it into use. That was the reason behind her cancer. The energy which is not used damages the body".

(How can it be put into use?)

"She must utilise her spiritual power."

(What does it entail?)

"Cleansing, Love and Compassion, Creativity"

(What is the purpose of the creativity?)

"Morale."

(Is it for herself?)

> *"What is for her is for others. You are not a blacksmith. You have all the power you need. There is love on the horizon."*

(Is it something positive in her personal life?)

> *"Yes, her essence is changing. It is the correct love, giving strength. All the others were desires of flesh."*

(Do you see anything regarding her professional life?)

> *"Morale. Once you have the strength, all will come into light. It is a matter of being in form."*

(Should she work on her own or with others?)

> *"Good to consider this. What the others can give you? God will open the doors."*

(Does she have the gifts of mediumship?)

> *"The important thing is the belief. She will mature further. Enlightenment comes through utilising logic."*

(Would it be useful to read some books?)

> *"The power is given from the Divine. Not all who read reach enlightenment."*

The second seance was held about two weeks later. We were told that we are now approaching the light.

(How are we to recognise 'the light'?)

> *"Two candle lights on a table."*

(Is it possible that the person can mislead herself?)

> *"How can you be happy but without knowing it? It is a gift from the Divine power. How can you not know Great happiness?"*

(Can she do something to receive it?)

"Everyone's duty is to bestow unconditional love. You cannot give what you are not destined to give. Do not be scared. You are in good health."

(What was the reason behind that lesson?)

"Superiority feelings. You then improved. What is superior is the spirit, not money or position. Suddenly you became aware. It would have been worse if you hadn't. Time is unlocking the way. You have good days to come. Do not be weak. All of your wishes will come true."

(Is the help for me or for the others around me?)

"There is only a short period. Don't exhaust yourself. Only the natural sugars should be consumed, such as honey. Accumulation of harmful acids change the nature of cells. Do not be pessimistic. The thoughts are both nectar and poison of the body."

(Any advice about my work?)

"Nothing is damaged. In fact, improved, provided that you do not allow your body to overrule your spirit."

(What does this mean?)

"You might go backwards. Put the spirit first."

(My brother is very distressed. Any way out for him?)

"The Divine gives difficulties to be a lesson. All difficulties lead to positive resolutions. Those who do not realise will make the journey longer. Know this, pity has no use. The Divine knows the misery of the sufferers. What you perceive as help may be in fact harmful."

He then advised that I choose certain foods which would support my health, such as okra, which is good for the immune system, parsley, currants and garlic. We were told that these should be consumed in whatever form we choose for the rest of all our lives.

The conversations above were an eye-opener for me, however limited my understanding was. Becoming aware of the Spirit world, with which we can communicate, influenced the next thirteen years of my life.

Shortly after my first communication with Ibn'i Sina, I started experimenting with automatic writing. It took a long time before I could make sense of the scribbles. In time, the writing became calmer and clearer. Once I could trust that it was not me writing, but the Spirit using my hand to give messages, I started hearing the Spirit; I could hear what the message was as I wrote it down.

It was as if words were preceding the writing — just as we all normally experience when we write anything down — except that in this case, I was writing words I had not thought of or had ever used in my daily life. But let me start at the beginning....

PART 1

EARLY EXPERIENCES

I was not a child who played with 'Spirit children' or saw or heard 'the Spirit'. I have no recollections of such experiences. My earliest memory of an unusual experience that I could not explain happened towards the end of high school.

We had to take exams in sports class just as we did in the academic subjects. Waiting in the garden of the high school to be examined, we decided to play leapfrog to pass the time. It went smoothly for a while until it was once again my turn to leap over one of the girls. I was tall but she was even taller. As I attempted my leap, my knees became stuck to her sides. I fell forward, face down, and in trying to protect myself, I badly injured my arms and knees. It was so serious a fall that I was excused from the exam.

The strange thing was that even today, all these years later, I still remember falling forward and seeing the floor coming up towards me as if in slow motion. Within those few seconds, I saw my whole life played backwards, very fast, as if on a tiny little screen in front of my eyes, and in full colour! At the time, I wondered if everyone who comes face to face with death has a similar experience but I did not research it. I now know it to have been a so-called a Near Death Experience, a phenomenon that has been widely investigated by medical science in recent years.

It was when I was in university that I started becoming aware that some of my intuitions were getting stronger, but still I paid no attention at all. For example, I could sense the intentions of people around me or I could pick up where certain people, to whom I felt close, were — even from a long distance. Looking back, I can see that my psychic senses were developing even if, at the time, I didn't fully appreciate what was happening.

I remember standing at the bottom of a very long road running up a steep hill, watching the cars coming down in the distance. Although I could not see the faces of either driver or passengers, I would somehow know who was in a particular car. When the car was near enough to see the people inside, I would turn out to be correct every time! I thought it was amusing that I should be able to do this, but nothing more.

It was the 1960s and we were living in Ankara. The capital city, Ankara was a small but, nevertheless, multi-cultural centre with all the embassies, the opera house, theatres and major universities. Among the young people, contemporary American and English pop music was popular. My brother was in a band; they had started by playing songs of Cliff Richard but soon Jimi Hendrix's psychedelic music replaced them. Bruce, an American friend who had recently moved to Turkey with his family, introduced us to smoking hashish and taking drugs. I still am not sure how many of the 'experiments' we did could qualify as 'spiritual', but what I can say is that some of them did feel like 'out of body' experiences.

On one occasion, we were gathered at a friend's house while her family was away when Bruce decided to swallow twenty cough tablets, apparently known as 'baby LSD' in the USA. The rest of us kept watch to ensure that they were as safe as he claimed. As he did not seem to come to any harm, the next day we all felt brave enough to experiment with the same pills. There were five of us, and soon the others seemed to be high, talking about the colour of the Bob Dylan music that was playing.

Nothing, however, seemed to be happening to me. Feeling rather upset, I was sitting on the floor next to them and listening to the music. Suddenly, I started seeing everything around me shimmering in a light tone of pink. Before I could utter a word, they all turned to me and said "Welcome Esi." I was now part of the group!

Looking back, I recall that all our experiments were born of a curiosity to see the results. It would take three or four hours before the effects of the drug would wear off and we could feel confident enough to go out — except that our pupils would be noticeably dilated for much longer. As a result, my brother and I had to sneak back home and go straight to our bedrooms so that we didn't arouse our parents' suspicions.

I remember one scene very clearly. We were listening to the music of Donovan. I cannot recall which song it was. All of a sudden, I was visualising a sandy beach at night with the waves moving softly in and out. The strange thing was that I felt that this whole scene was me, and the music of Donovan was the moonlight upon me.

Our experiments with hashish and drugs lasted only a short time, at least for me. Soon after, I left for Sydney, Australia. As for my brother, I heard that he had started smoking in his room at home but my parents found out. That put a stop to his adventures.

Some twenty years later, in 1988, I was living and working in London when I heard that my grandmother had broken her hip. She was 89 years old and one of the most important people in my life. By the time she reached the age of 49 she had lost her husband, a daughter and a son. She lived with us while my brother and I were very young, helping my parents to care for us. She then lived with my aunt and uncle, and helped them to raise their two sons. Throughout my life I spent most of my summer holidays with my grandmother in Istanbul.

While she was in bed with a broken hip, I would call her almost every day to find out how she was. Finally, I arranged for my summer holiday and bought my airline ticket to go to Istanbul to see her. My flight was booked for a Saturday. On the Tuesday night before, I had a dream; in it, I heard my mother very clearly saying "Esi, come here tomorrow!"

I woke up feeling anxious. I was not sure whether I'd really had the dream and if I should act on it. But I decided that since travelling on Thursday would make only one day's difference, I did not change my ticket. My grandmother died on Friday. By the time I arrived on Saturday, her funeral already taken place so I never saw her again.

Years later, in 1995, I had a similar dream. This time I was living and working in Brunei, Borneo. I saw a television screen going fuzzy. It then cleared and I saw my father saying, "My dear daughter, do come over as soon as possible" before the screen went fuzzy again. I woke up feeling anxious and, having learned something from the previous experience, I immediately requested time off for an early summer holiday from the office, and flew to Istanbul. My father seemed perfectly well, so I mentioned the dream and teased him, saying that he'd made me come over early! I spent a lovely summer holiday with my parents, after which I returned to work in Borneo.

My father passed into spirit in 1998, aged 76. He had skin cancer, which he found out about a year after my dream. I now understand that the dream was his plea for me to return to live and work in Istanbul so that we could spend our last few years together. Sadly, neither he nor I understood it at the time.

Two years after the dream, my partner and I travelled to Istanbul from Hong Kong, where I was living, for our Christmas holiday. By that time, we knew about my father's melanoma but thought it was being managed. We spent a lovely Christmas Eve at home. In the morning, my father started haemorrhaging internally and was rushed to the hospital. It turned out that the pain-killers he had been taking were to blame.

I extended my stay in Istanbul and travelled by ferry to the hospital every day. Towards the end, he seemed to be sleeping most of the time and, occasionally, having a conversation with some children he appeared to be seeing. As I had not yet started communicating with the Spirit, I was not sure although I hoped that he was being visited by the Spirit.

On the day he died, about half way through the ferry crossing, I suddenly became aware that a popular children's song was being played over the speakers particularly loudly. It was usually a rather quiet journey and so I was startled, but also pleasantly surprised: my father had written the lyrics. The song had won a children's song competition organised by the Turkish Radio and Television Corporation for UNESCO's International Year of the Child in 1979.

Later during the day, I was sitting and quietly chatting with my mother and brother next to my father's bed in the hospital. He appeared to be asleep. He then opened his eyes and turned his face away from us when I realised that something was different and shouted for the nurse. Shortly after, he drew his last breath. We were all shocked. I hugged my father for the last time and, a few seconds later, I felt as if I was being hugged back in return. In those few seconds, it felt as if I was filled up by this enormous love and I could now let him go.

My father's passing into spirit had a devastating effect on my mother. She cried every day for about two years and lost interest in life in general. All she wanted was to die like my father! This seemed to be the beginning of the dementia that came a few years later, followed by a skin condition that could be managed only with steroids.

She was unwell for almost six years before she passed into spirit, spending most of the day in bed, being nursed by a carer, and receiving occasional visits from my brother who also lived in Istanbul. At regular intervals, she would be taken to the hospital for observation. My trips to Istanbul were becoming more frequent in order to manage her care better. About a year before her passing I was with her and I realised that she was seeing the Spirit.

We moved her bed into the living room so that she would not be left on her own throughout the day. One morning, I was alone with her and while I was sitting at the table, having breakfast and checking my emails, she suddenly asked who the young child standing next to me was. I did not want to worry her by showing that I was surprised by her question, so I casually asked, as if too busy to check for myself, "boy or girl, mother?" She said a little boy. "What is his name?" I asked, to which she replied "Ali." Then she said, "Give him some breakfast too"!

I was so pleased to hear her comment. I already knew (having been so informed by another medium in London) that I have a little cheeky boy who sometimes works with me. I now knew that my mother would not feel alone and does have company!

In between my trips, I would call the carer from London to check on things. The last time I called, I immediately knew that my mother had to be admitted to the hospital. I asked her to inform my brother and call the ambulance urgently. The next morning, I spoke to her doctor who confirmed that my mother's health was deteriorating. Without delay, I bought my ticket for the afternoon flight.

It was 17 July 2012, and we were due to land in Istanbul around 10.00pm. It would have taken me another hour or so to go to the hospital. I did not know if she was still conscious and whether she had been told that I was flying in to see her. But I did not want my mother to suffer in case she was waiting and holding on until my arrival. Half way during the flight I talked to her in my mind. I told her "please do not wait for me if you are ready and wanting to go".

We landed on schedule. I called the carer at the hospital before I left the airport. She informed me that my mother had passed into spirit just a short while before. So I never saw her again.

A few months later, I received a message from my mother through another medium at a church service. The message was that my mother wanted me to know that her passing was very peaceful, having heard my whispering in her ear!

1- LEARNING TO QUIETEN MY MIND

In 1994 I was invited to join a local design office in Brunei. It is a tiny country with less than 6,000 square kilometres of land and is located on the northwest coast of the island of Borneo in the South China Sea. At the time, the population was only 260,000 people. Brunei is mainly a collection of small pockets of settlements, mostly on the banks of a river, within a largely virgin jungle. Its capital, Bandar Seri Begawan, is located on the banks of Brunei River where it meets the ocean. While it took us less than two hours to drive from one end of the country to the other along the coastline, the jungle extends inland quite a long distance. The only way to reach most of the tribal settlements is by water taxi, which we often used for our jungle expeditions.

I worked for a locally owned company as an architect and urban designer. We had been commissioned to design projects for the Sultan's brother. My last project was to design a new town. The Sultan was building a new hotel on the coast and a golf course up on the hills. It was thought that the latter would generate such interest that the wealthy population of South East Asia might choose to own their own houses in the area. It was a design challenge as there was not even an existing village on which to base the town. However, I was happy with my design and I heard that so were they. I left Brunei shortly after.

To start with it was lovely to be living in such a lush environment with temperatures between 28-33 degrees C throughout the year. I had to drive to work, then to a construction site for lunch, and back to work and finally home — all of which added up to almost 100 kilometres a day. It was part of the daily routine to see families of monkeys or big monitor lizards while driving and having to stop to allow them to cross the road.

There were various groups of ex-pats; mainly doctors, teachers, designers, and pilots from different nationalities working there. It was a safe environment for families with young children. Most single people spent weekends at the beach or the yacht club, or travelling to nearby countries or islands. Brunei is wedged in between Malaysian Sabah and Sarawak, which were easy to reach for day trips.

My parents visited at the beginning of 1995, and stayed with me for a month. My father drew a collection of caricatures showing his character *Mr Foreigner*'s impressions of the country. Some of these were later published in the Royal Brunei Airlines magazine, *Muhibah* (November/December 1995) and also in the weekend travel supplement of a newspaper in Turkey. Looking back, I appreciate how lucky I was to have had the opportunity to work in this tiny country and how precious the memories of my parent's visit.

Having lived and worked in this amazing green jungle environment for more than a year, I went to visit friends in Hong Kong, where I was struck by the contrast! Hong Kong Island was another kind of jungle — but one of concrete with buildings rising some 45 floors. It is an incredibly busy and lively place to live in. The main island is basically a very steep rock with a very narrow shoreline, and densely populated.

Shortly after, I was offered a position with a private planning company in Hong Kong, which I accepted, and moved there the end of 1995. At the time the new airport was not yet completed, so airliners flew into the mainland to land, weaving through the high buildings. My first impression of Hong Kong was 'how exciting to be back in an urban environment'! My parents again visited me in Hong Kong and this time his impressions of the place were exhibited at the sports club in Discovery Bay. Here are two of them.

2- Two impressions of Hong Kong through the eyes of Mr F

I lived on Lantau Island, which is also very mountainous with steep high hills. At the time, there were no road or train connections to the rest of Hong Kong and so, as a result, there were no cars on the island — just golf buggies used by those who lived up on the hills.

I met my partner shortly afterwards through work and he moved in with me. My flat was on the eighth floor of a residential building by the sea, overlooking the bay. The living room gave the feeling, almost, of being on the deck of a ship as the walls forming the two sides of the room were full-height glass. The eighth floor was the highest I could agree to live on; any higher, and I could not relate to the people on the street and felt completely cut off.

Residents of the island had to take a half-hour ferry trip to the main island for work. It did not sound very practical to start with, but the return trip to the island was so relaxing. By the time I would arrive at home, my work-related concerns would be pushed to the back of my mind and lose all their importance. Once you stepped off the boat, you would find yourself in the environment of a seaside resort. Next to the port was the square — full of outdoor tables surrounded by shops and restaurants on three sides with a sports club at the far end. Behind the square was the beach, where the local sailing club was situated.

At the weekends, we went sailing or hiking on the very steep hills surrounding the bay or on the main island. During the week, I either went to the gym or to play squash and once a week to yoga. Previously, while living in the UK, I had friends who did yoga, but somehow I was not interested, nor was I interested in meditation. The idea of sitting in a fixed position and humming words I found incomprehensible did not appeal to me. Now, looking back, I see that working in Hong Kong and starting to do yoga was the reason I became interested in learning meditation.

Yoga classes were given in the primary school in the evenings. Hot and humid days turned into much more pleasant and balmy evenings most of the year. The room in which we had our classes would have all the windows open and you could hear the sounds of crickets outside.

The short meditation we were asked to do at the end was very relaxing and it encouraged me to consider taking meditation classes. I found a class given by a Swiss woman living up on the hills. I took her classes for over a year and I enjoyed it very much. It was very different from what I expected. She would guide our meditation and, more importantly, she also taught us how to breathe correctly.

Through meditation, I became aware that our world is full of noise even when it is at its quietest because our heads are full of thoughts, questions, plans and replays of events in our daily lives. Once I developed further and became familiar with the relaxation of my physical body, I no longer needed to follow the guidance given for the meditation but would quickly go into a very deep relaxation — both physically and mentally. As I became more and more experienced, so the lasting effect of the deep peaceful state would continue for longer and longer.

After a while, the time spent in meditation became my most restful and energising state of being. I learned that by quietening our minds we eventually become aware of our own souls.

I remember walking back from a deep relaxation and meditation session one evening. The classes were held at the teacher's flat up on the hill and I lived within walking distance, by the sea. As I walked, the thought of a recent argument I'd had with my partner came into my mind. I was suddenly extremely sad and tears started falling down my cheeks. The amazing thing was that at the same time as I was feeling the pain, I also felt so detached from my body that it was as if I was watching myself feeling the sadness from outside of myself. I recall saying to myself, "See, that is what sadness is."

Working and living in Hong Kong kept me very busy. I had moved there because I'd been offered a job as the principal urban designer by a private planning office. The projects we were involved with were mostly commissioned by the Hong Kong Planning Department. However, after a year, I began to feel rather frustrated because the partners of the company treated Urban Design not as a design tool but as a graphics exercise. I therefore decided to seek alternative employment.

Fortunately, I was offered a place with an architectural company owned by an Australian architect, where I became involved in very large-scale projects in Burma, the Philippines and China. I mostly did the designs for proposals or competitions. This time, it was the pressure put on the design team, and the very long hours, which made it frustrating and tiring. However, in the meantime, I began to receive requests from other consultancy companies to do urban design consultancy and environmental impact studies for them. So once again, I left the company but this time I started working freelance.

But those were not the only changes taking place at the time. I had been 'talking' to the Spirit whenever I felt bored or thought I needed some advice!

It started before my move to Borneo. I started experimenting with automatic writing after I was introduced to the Spirit in 1987, but it was mostly illegible scribbles, with sometimes only one or two words I could decipher. In the early 1990s I started 'hearing' the messages and soon, these messages turned into conversations. I was not sure whom I was communicating with. It felt as if I was sitting on a street corner and people passing by would talk to me. I could just about hear that there were sometimes different 'voices' but could not be sure.

Nevertheless, it was convenient and useful for me as my work required me to travel extensively. Having someone to talk to during these flights or car rides was most welcome; it was like having an invisible friend along with me. I was soon being told what to expect within a short time, for example, someone coming to visit me, or a present to be received. These predictions all came true!

Slowly, I started trusting and relying on the Spirit to tell me what to expect or what to do. It even reached the stage at which I was checking with them if I needed to take my umbrella with me before leaving the flat! But then it started going wrong! I would invest all my trust in them for some major decisions in life only to find out that I was misled! Only then was I told that they are in the spirit world and it is me on earth that needs to learn from my experiences. It is my life and I must make my own choices. Otherwise, my life would be wasted.

It was good to have 'invisible friends' to make me feel that I was not on my own. Looking back, I also realise that all the physical activities, such as trekking up and down the hills in the evenings or weekends, sailing and meditation, helped me to stay connected to nature for the four and a half years I lived in Hong Kong. It would have been very easy to get carried away by the materialistic world that Hong Kong offered, compared to the other parts of the world I had lived in.

In Hong Kong, people are extremely business oriented and they work very long hours throughout the year. At the time, it seemed as if all the local young people wanted was to grow up and wear Calvin Klein. Everybody looked the same. It could be that I felt this because I did not speak or understand Cantonese or Mandarin, yet I worked with some local professionals in the office, with whom I shared a common language, but their attitude to life did not appear to be any different.

I did not know what to expect from living in Hong Kong. All I knew was I just moved from one extreme environment in Borneo to another in Hong Kong. However, working in Hong Kong did offer better opportunities for travel and more income, but did not feed into my expectation of finding 'meaning in my life' or a place for myself in the world. It was not a conscious decision at the time. I firmly believe that travelling and experiencing different cultures makes you a richer person in every way. You learn that there are a variety of ways of doing the same thing and that one is not necessarily better than the other. It makes you aware that we always have choices in life. But after four and a half years in Hong Kong, I knew it was time to go back to Europe.

2- A NEW DOOR OPENING

As is usually the case with Spirit, new opportunities open up in front of us when we are ready. It is then up to us whether we enter those doors or not.

At the end of 1999, I returned from the Far East to the UK and started looking for a job. In fact, I was torn and could not make up my mind whether I should be moving back to Istanbul or staying in London. That was where my flat was and I had already spent 23 years away from Istanbul. Having lost my father two years earlier, my mother was putting pressure on me to return home, but I decided to wait and see where my next job would be offered.

I wrote to some of the large architectural design companies in London and was invited for interviews by most of them. Most said they were curious to see what kind of person I was with such a curriculum vitae! But none offered a job. In addition, I put my name down with two agencies but, again, neither returned with any interviews.

I was in my one-bedroom flat in Hampstead, living on my savings. However, as the time went by and no job offers came, I started to feel less confident. It seemed that I was 'over qualified' with 'too much international experience'! I was trying to justify thinking that it would be difficult to find a senior position as a designer; they would not be willing to pay high salaries to someone they do not know well, even though they seemed to be impressed with me in the interviews. I started feeling rather upset and depressed. It was another few years before I found out why!

With this diminished prospect of finding employment, I had to sell my flat and found a much cheaper one in Kilburn. It was the first time I'd tackled an old Victorian house conversion and the challenge appealed to me. My flat was on the top floor and it took me six months to design and carry out the complete refurbishment. I had always enjoyed being on a construction site, but in this instance I was not familiar with the structure of these old buildings and, in addition, I was responsible for finding and supervising tradesmen and engineers.

The flat turned out to be my learning curve on the construction of Victorian buildings as well as a reference for future refurbishment projects. Soon, without having set out to do so, I was being asked by more and more people who'd heard about it by word of mouth to do refurbishments for them. I was being looked after!

Working freelance and with so much free time on my hands gave me the opportunity to take part in different activities. In 2000, I became a member of the Heath Hands, a voluntary organisation working with the City of London Corporation and English Heritage staff members on the conservation and maintenance of Hampstead Heath. The weekly sessions involved working on the Heath with the rangers and conservation officers, and the activity is something I still do after all these years. I was also invited to join the Hampstead Conservation Committee Planning Group to review planning applications made to the Borough of Camden.

But, most significantly, soon after moving back to London, I found out about a Spiritualist Church near Notting Hill Gate, called the London Spiritual Mission. I do not recall how I found out about it; it may be that a friend asked me to go along to one of the services. Not being a religious person, I did not know much about the church services. Previously, I'd visited only to view the buildings as an architect or to sit quietly to contemplate. Until that time, I did not know anything about Spiritualism; actually I did not even know that there was a movement called Spiritualism, let alone about 600 Spiritualist churches or centres in the UK!

I've never thought of myself as belonging to any religion. In fact, I did not like and still do not like or support the idea of 'religions'. However, I was curious.

Having been 'talking' to the Spirit for a long time, I found it fascinating to witness that the mediums appeared to be communicating with the dead relatives and friends of people who attended Spiritualist services. I always thought that we on earth and those in Spirit were two separate communities: we humans without many choices in our lives, born to families, countries, and societies we did not choose and then died, and that was the end of it! Spirit on the other hand, appeared to be all-knowing, wise, and separate! How wrong I was!

I started going to the services and watching people receiving messages. I did not receive any for some time! Then one day, I received a message from my ex-father-in-law. I was fond of him and I found the whole experience extremely emotional. It was as though someone travelled to a place where he now lives, met him, and brought back his loving messages. I suddenly received messages from someone whom I thought had disappeared forever!

Most of the Spiritualist churches have two services a week; usually one during the week and at least one on Sundays. One Wednesday evening, I arrived early at the London Spiritual Mission. There were not yet many people. I sat behind a woman and we soon started to talk. I found out that she was a ballerina from Portugal and had been visiting this church for a long time and also that she attended the development classes it ran. As we were chatting, the church secretary walked by and stopped to say hello to my acquaintance, who introduced us. I enquired about the development groups and expressed my interest in joining one. She took my details and two months later I was invited to join them.

3- DISCOVERING GIFTS

As much as going to Spiritualist churches and finding out that there are hundreds of them in the UK, as well as many centres or community centres where mediums demonstrate their gifts, joining a Closed Circle was an eye opener for me.

The most important realisation for me was to come to the understanding that we, as humans, and Spirit are not two different beings; we, here on earth, are spirits too. The difference is that we have bodies as we have temporarily chosen to play different personalities in an 'earth school' for our spiritual development. Death, therefore, is nothing more than a shedding of our bodies when the time comes! Life is eternal and communication with those who have passed into spirit is possible!

Because I'd been brought up by scientific parents, these were not concepts that I could readily accept. It took me more than three years of sitting in a Closed Circle and experimenting with the group to accept them as the truth nobody talks about.

Initially, an important part of the development was disciplining myself to learn how to quieten my mind. This I had already started doing in Hong Kong in meditation classes, where I found out that by quietening my mind, I could feel and hear my own soul. Joining the Closed Circle, I realised that previously I had done meditations only when I was in class but had not made it part of my daily routine. I now had to discipline myself to do just that, which I discovered made it much easier to tune into the Spirit. The next important step was to learn to trust the communication received.

I really did not have any idea about what to expect from a Closed Circle when I first joined the group. I would now recommend anyone seriously interested in developing their sensitivity to join a traditional Closed Circle rather than going to three-monthly classes. The traditional circles are usually open ended. We are all at different stages of our spiritual development on earth; therefore it is an advantage if you are part of a group of people whose energies you share for a long period, and to experiment with them.

It is very important that one feels comfortable with the leader of the Circle. I strongly believe that the leader is there, firstly, to ensure a secure environment for everyone, but also to instil discipline within the group. By this I mean not to 'teach' how to communicate, because we all learn how to develop and communicate with the Spirit from our own guides. It is almost like 'downloading' a language of communication from them. As we are all different and have different guides helping us, that language would be different for each one of us.

Also, we take what we see in our daily lives so much for granted as the only reality, unaware that what we see is just our individual reality of the world. Our 'reality' is shaped by our own experiences in life, and therefore it is natural that we perceive what we expect to perceive and interpret it accordingly. In other words, it is like looking at the world through spectacles we deliberately wear: if the lenses are pink, we see, hear, feel the world as pink! As with everything in life, we need to widen our experiences if we want to widen our perceptions. The more we widen our experiences, whether by reading, studying or travelling, etc., the richer we become.

So, it is largely who we are that determines who we communicate in Spirit with and how we communicate. As in life, we seem to attract in Spirit those whose life experiences and families we can have empathy with. Therefore, the group members should not be put under pressure to act like or talk like the leader or anyone else. It must be accepted and respected that all mediums work in different ways.

Joining a group does not presuppose that you want to become, or indeed will become, a platform medium. The most important point about joining is to develop your own spiritual awareness and then your gifts. Whether you choose to share them with others, as I do, is a decision only you can take. It is also your privilege not to take the last step.

I attended the Closed Circle every week, for three and a half years, never missing any of the meetings unless I was away overseas.

At the start of the Circle, the leader would say a short prayer, including a reference to the intention of the group gathered for development. The next step would be to encourage everyone to relax by going through a relaxation and meditation exercise.

Some newcomers may, at first, find difficulty in following either the relaxation or the guided meditation, or it might be simply that they did not easily appreciate that they would physically feel different when deeply relaxed. However, by sharing their experiences at the end of the session, everyone soon learns what to look for in their own body. Once you become aware of the changes in your own body, you start enjoying the experience.

You may soon start experiencing different sensations in your body; it may be that parts or all of your body become heavier and heavier in a most comfortable way, so much so that you do not feel your body after a while. You may feel that you have become so much lighter without the conscious weight of your physical body. Some mediums, when working with a group of people, call it 'sitting in the power' when you do not need to be guided but sit quietly within the energy of the group, deeply relaxed.

Within the Circle, it is important to learn the difference between Psychic and Spiritual mediums and those who already have these gifts. As I understand it, we all have layers of energy that we carry with us. Just outside our physical body is the etheric energy body, which carries all we experience as much as all that we relate to in our daily lives. In other words, we carry all of our 'factual information' around our physical selves. Based on these, we also project the possible futures in store for us. A good Psychic medium would be able to pick up this information from the etheric body and give us these details. This kind of sensitivity is something we all have, but most of us have neither developed it nor even become aware of it. This is a popular gift as it helps the Psychic to give 'readings' for our possible future. Of course, there is degree of interpretation and it is not a communication with the Spirit.

Spirit communication, on the other hand, is basically communicating with a person who has 'died' and passed into Spirit. Once I could accept the fact that we can communicate with people who have passed into Spirit, I realised that any evidence that can be given to the person they are related to, or know, is of the utmost importance.

Moreover, it seems to me essential that this evidence should be specific to the person or to a memory, rather than being of a general kind of information that could be applied to most people. For example, "the lady communicating is your grandmother and she cooked lots of food and cakes," would seem to be too general. Depending on the gift or capability of the medium, it would be best if names, personalities and specific memories could be given as the evidence.

Our leader was Steve Lamont. He was a very disciplined but fair leader. As any serious leader would do, his first concern was to provide us with a safe environment. He would lock the door at 7.00 pm and not allow anybody in if they were late. I did not appreciate it until one day when one of the group members started coughing violently and the sound was almost like a physical pain entering my body. With the deep meditation, I did not know that all my five senses were to become extremely heightened.

Steve would also make sure that he gave a voice to each one of us during the meetings. He gave clear guidance and allowed us to experiment. Steve never made us feel that he or his guides were in charge and knew it all. In three and a half years, his guide wanted to talk to us directly only once. We were asked to consider if we would seriously like to take the responsibility to work with Spirit. We did not have to say it aloud but make up our minds quietly. I remember saying a BIG "yes!"

As a group, we demonstrated individually on the Open Platform of the London Mission and also started visiting other Open Platforms for fledglings in other churches. After three and a half years, Steve told me that I was ready to go onto 'the platform', which is the commonly used phrase for standing in front of a crowd to demonstrate.

When I joined the Closed Circle, I could already 'hear' the Spirit. It was interesting that once I could tune into the Spirit, I lost my ability to 'hear' for a while and started 'seeing'. That was followed by 'feeling' the Spirit. The experimentation with different gifts was in fact a way of experimenting with our guides to learn what to expect when communicating with them, almost like downloading a very special language into our sensitivities. Sometimes, for some of us, they all emerged together.

We all have five senses; sight, sound, touch, smell and taste, and we learn how to use them from birth. Unless we are taught, we are not aware that it is not the individual organs doing different functions on their own but acting as a specialised system and working in unison with the brain. All we see, hear, taste, smell and feel is in fact the product of our brain and the central nervous system.

I now feel very comfortable to accept the theory that spiritual mediumship is 'mind to mind'. My own experiences convinced me that any image, thought, sensation, sound, feeling and even memory of a specific event that may be received in the mind of the medium forms in their consciousness as part of the communication.

In the next pages, I share some of my early learning experiments. They taught me how to make use of the visual information I was given.

SEEING THE EVIDENCE (CLAIRVOYANCE)

In one of the early experiments in the Closed Circle, I saw two people in my mind's eye; a man and a woman who turned out to be the parents of someone in the group. My link with her parents was purely visual. I could describe the couple: how they were dressed, how they carried themselves, how the father had a habit of sitting with his legs apart with his arms over his knees, and his manner of talking. I could also describe the environment they were living in — they were from a Caribbean island. It felt amazing to meet someone new in the group, yet to know so much about her dead parents!

In another experiment, I tuned into a woman but I 'saw' her only from her chest to her nose. She was dressed in black with a small collar, buttoned up, almost like a Victorian mistress. Her hair was pulled back tightly into a bun. Her mouth was tightly closed, indicating someone who was a disciplinarian or critical of others. Her very straight neck expressed her mannerisms and very strict adherence to rules. I could then describe the person's personality based on these visual clues.

I sometimes receive information in the form of visual images in my mind. I call it *seeing in my mind's eye*. I do not know how else to describe it except to say that it is like remembering being with them at a specific place and time, and the image appears to me as very real. This definitely reinforces the notion that our communication is 'mind to mind'.

The visual images I receive may be in the form of pictures (as in a photograph) or scenes (as in a film). What is conveyed can be either part of their memories, such as if they lived by the sea and had a sailing boat, or it can be a scene capturing the essential information that would be acceptable as evidence, such as someone shown walking along the corridor in a nursing home, or on a stretcher being rushed into the hospital.

Having tuned into their mind and they in turn having tuned into mine, any specific memory they recall would, for me, be like seeing it in my mind's eye as if I shared the memory with them. This form of communication is called *clairvoyance* — clear seeing.

As in the physical world, appearances also tell us a lot about the people we are seeing. Even 'seeing' only a small part of the body can reveal a lot about the person — for instance their sense of dress, age, wealth, health, and so on.

Of course, it can also be symbols that we see, which sometimes require interpretation either by the medium or the recipient. It may be that the symbol has a fairly commonly held meaning, for example, it may be a symbol with the colours of a football team, a school or a region of the country. In that case it may help the medium to identify where the person is from. But sometimes, the image may be given as a short-cut for the recipient: based on the memories of the person, the symbol may have a meaning for them, for example it might refer to a place they went for holiday or where they worked together.

FEELING OR SENSING THE EVIDENCE (CLAIRSENTIENCE)

As mentioned above, spiritual mediumship is a mental mediumship; all messages are communicated mind-to-mind between the communicator and the medium. To me, this clearly indicates that our consciousness — which holds our memories, experiences and knowledge gained during our lives — belongs to the soul, not the physical brain. This is how it is possible for people to communicate with us after death. In other words, if consciousness resided in the physical brain, then it would be lost forever with the death of the brain.

In the case of information being conveyed in the form of feelings and sensations through the brain, the information may be interpreted by the medium as if they are their own 'feelings'. In mediumistic language the information received in the form of feelings or sensations is called c*lairsentience* — clear sensing evidence — and the mediums are said to be working as clairsentients.

The information conveyed by 'feeling or sensing' may be emotional as well as physical. In other words, while the feelings may be those of joy or sadness, they can also be a physical touch on the head or shoulder, a pain like a headache, or the touch of a sharp object. It can also be a motion. I clearly remember the first time this happened to me, as it was a completely new physical experience for me. It happened when we were in the Closed Circle. Usually, there would be about eight to ten of us in the Circle, and each of us would take turns to exercise by linking to a Spirit relating to someone in the group. My link was to one of the men. Soon after I started the communication, I felt that I had to move my arm and fingers as if I was cutting something and then, I needed to move my arm as if I was drawing large circles. The person I was doing the sitting for smiled and told us that his father was a tailor and his grandfather would do the patterns!

On another occasion when I was given clairsentient evidence, the recipient asked if I could qualify how the person died. Usually mediums do not like to enter into conversations during a demonstration because this could interfere with the process and they may start interpreting the information or even try to meet the expectations of the recipient. However, in this case, even before I had a chance to repeat the question, I felt a sharp pain in my stomach and had to bend over. The recipient smiled sadly at me and said "that is right, he went to the USA on a visit and while there, he was shot in the stomach."

It is only by trusting our communication skills with the Spirit that we can pass on the messages that are conveyed to us. As in this story, the physical pain can also be transferred as a physical sensation. However, I find that we all have one or two senses stronger than others and we tend to employ, and may even express ourselves with, these senses in our daily lives.

I became aware of this when I started experimenting with the different senses. I realised that when working on my architectural projects, I usually talked about the 'feeling of the spaces' rather than the physical dimensions of size or proportions to describe them. Today, although I use all my senses in my communications, I find it easier picking up 'feelings' from the communicator.

One important aspect I should mention is that the developing medium should be encouraged to *ask* for more information from the Spirit during the communication rather than *wait* for the Spirit to supply them with it.

It is also true that giving information about the personality of the communicator provides much better evidence than giving, for example, their height or weight, because those can be relative values. For example, to a tall person, most people would be short; similarly, most people would be overweight to a skinny person. However, describing someone as nervous or shy or as a larger-than-life character might be easier to identify the person with.

A most amazing communication I had at the beginning of my development was one in which the person in spirit conveyed different emotions, all relating to a particular situation he was in.

I was visiting Istanbul in June 2004 when a friend said that she would like to introduce me to a group of her friends who were interested in my work. This was before I had started sketching spirit portraits. I went to her place, where I found about ten people. I talked about my experiences and explained how I worked. They all wanted me to illustrate with a demonstration.

As soon as I felt that I had a connection with someone in spirit and I 'knew' that he was a man, I also started having difficulty in breathing. The first impression was that I had been running and, therefore, was out of breath. Then, suddenly, something made me feel very scared. My breathing was becoming more and more laboured. I then heard myself saying "they will never find me!"

I asked the communicator to give me further information about himself and the person he was wishing to connect to. I repeated the name I heard, and he said he was a school friend to someone in the room. They were six years old when they met and their homes were next door to each other. They used to play Cowboys and Indians. By that time, I noticed that a young man in the room was smiling. He acknowledged the person communicating, their friendship, and the games they played.

I then felt that I had to stand and bow to everyone (as an actor does at the end of a play). The young man accepting the information said "that is how he would withdraw from a room!" He then told us the friend's story, which was that he had gone on a skiing holiday with two other friends. They were around 18 years old. While skiing there was an avalanche and they were all were buried under the snow. Only one was found alive and, yes, the person communicating was never found!

HEARING THE EVIDENCE (CLAIRAUDIENCE)

My communication with Spirit started with automatic writing. The letters were small and almost illegible at first. Then they became larger and more clear and my writing felt more confident. It was only later on, as I did the automatic writing, that I also started 'hearing' the Spirit. I sometimes still revert to this method I employ whenever I find it difficult to hear them. Some call it hearing with the 'inner ear'.

In my experience, if someone is communicating with me for the first time, 'hearing' him or her is usually somewhat difficult. I believe the reason lies not only on our part but also on their part. An explanation was given to me some time ago and I go along with it: because we, as humans, are part of the material world, our vibrations are very slow. Those in spirit are pure energy, and therefore their rate of vibrating is extremely fast. In order to communicate, we need to learn to increase the vibration of our energies while they too need to learn to lower theirs — so we can meet half way. This has been confirmed to me by the Spirit many times. New communicators often say that they are going to get used to communicating with us and will be better at it soon!

During the time that I could only hear the Spirit, I did not really pay too much attention to who they were. I remember asking once and the reply was "it is not important!" However, once I developed my gifts and started communicating for others, it became important that the person in Spirit should be identified. In this context, the names, if given, would be clear evidence. However, names can also be misleading, as we may not necessarily remember them immediately. More about that later.

'Hearing' the voices does not mean hearing only the spoken words. 'Hearing' also means being able to identify characteristics such as the manner of speaking and the sound of the voice, etc. Such details are also helpful as a way of recognising the communicator; therefore, it should be considered important evidence. The sound and the tone of the voice, which may be, for instance, high pitched or very soft, or their manner of speaking, for example, very fast with a nervous energy, or a laughing lilt, etc., can provide us with sufficient evidence by which to recognise them. In fact this is often the case because we remember people not as in pictures but mostly because of these individual characteristics. I remember an occasion, at the end of a workshop I attended at the College of Psychic Studies (CPS) a long time ago, when I was invited to demonstrate my gifts. I had a link with a gentleman with a distinctive baritone voice together with a serious manner of talking even when he teased people, and he was easily recognised by a lady, much like the one in the following communication.

"KNOWING" THE EVIDENCE (CLAIRCOGNISANCE)

This form of communication is the most difficult to explain as the only way I can describe it is as a feeling "that I just know!" I find that this kind of communication is not usually the main source of mental conversation that I have with the Spirit but something given as an "add-on" — by way of an impression — to that which I have already received by other means. I usually find that 'I know' and I pass on these extra bits of knowledge when I give information on their memories or messages in the form of ideas, thoughts, or concepts. For example getting the impression that someone does not like dogs, or certain types of drink or food. This form of communication is usually called *claircognisance*.

During a demonstration, if I feel that I need to express something because I know it to be true, I will do so. However, this is easier said than done in my case. In my daily life in England, I do not think in my mother tongue, I think in English. Many of my verbal responses to events are instinctive and automatically would be expressed in English. However, because sometimes, 'knowing' something is more subtle, it requires me to think and identify what it is and in these cases I am generally thinking in my mother tongue. Even after so many years of living in the UK, I may sometimes find it difficult to translate into the right words or expression in English.

It is probably easier to illustrate — rather than explain — so here follows one of my early communications as medium, taken from my notes:

After my Closed Circle ended, I wanted to see how some of the other development groups worked, and so I joined monthly advanced classes at the College of Psychic Studies. In early 2004, I was in Ian Hunter's class, where I was giving a message to a woman from her husband. The communication was part visual, part knowing, and part hearing. As this was a relatively complicated piece of mediumship, and it was quite early in my development, I was gratified that Ian commented afterwards that it had been "excellent mediumship," using the various forms of communication.

> *ME: "Your husband is here. He is a big man but does not have very large shoulders. He does not usually wear a jacket but when he does, it is rather tight around shoulders. He did not wear dark blue or black jackets with white shirts but chose brown and tobacco colours".*
>
> *RECIPIENT: "Very true"*

ME: *"He was not a person who drank much water".*

RECIPIENT: *"No, he used to say he would rust if he drank water!'"*

ME: *"He was not much of a dog person. He did not mind if there were cats around. He would like it if a bird rested on his hand but did not want to care for one".*

RECIPIENT: *"No, he rather believed in working dogs."*

ME: *"He would talk to people but then he would switch off. He was not one who would socialise all the time".*

RECIPIENT: *"No"*

ME: *"He is looking down, and says 'I was the one who remembered the anniversaries, not her'".*

RECIPIENT: *[She jumps] "That is not true."*

ME: *"It seems he is teasing you because after he said that he raised his eye brows and looked at you".*

RECIPIENT: *"That is what I liked about him. He would say something and I would react before it registered and he would look at me like that."*

ME: *"He is showing himself in a place like a shop front. A room on the street level with panelled windows. The wood is painted a reddish colour, and the entry is on the left hand corner".*

RECIPIENT: *[She smiles] "Yes"*

ME: *"I am not sure if this is symbolic but he is hugging his hands as if he is getting ready to 'meet' clients or the public. He shows great confidence and says 'the show is starting' as if he has been getting ready for a long time".*

RECIPIENT: *"Yes, I can take that."*

ME: *"I feel he wants to give you confidence and show how ready you are. Please also take his love".*

CHANNELLING MESSAGES

Channelling is the term used when the medium allows the Spirit to use his/her own voice to directly communicate the Spirit's own words. Because English is not my mother tongue, I was initially shy and reluctant to let myself channel. My first channelling experience was in May 2003, when a short poetic message was given — in English! I noted it down after the Closed Circle, and here it is:

"To give light

You have to learn to give

To learn to give, you have to open your heart

Let people see it is full of love

Let them see themselves in your heart

So they trust

That's when they are ready to receive

That's when you give light".

CHANNELLING DRAWINGS

It was towards the end of my development in the Closed Circle that I started channelling drawings. I noticed it at first when I felt the urge to doodle tiny sketches. At first they looked a little like 'faces' but I was not sure as I really did not expect to be drawing portraits.

However, as I was used to doing automatic writing, I felt comfortable letting the pencil lead. The faces started appearing; the early ones were not very clear, as shown in this drawing I made in November 2002.

3- An early sketch

These tiny drawings of faces with many lines started getting larger and clearer in time. As I was not sketching anyone that I could see, I knew that the Spirit was sketching these portraits. I continued sketching when I visited other spiritualist church services during other mediums' demonstrations.

It was not until 2004 when it was proven to me that the portraits are real 'hard evidence'. The proof seemed completely obvious when I received a photograph of a person I had drawn!

Even as an architect, I had not done any free-hand drawings or paintings for such a long time. When visiting art exhibitions, I find that the smell of oil paintings conjures up nostalgic memories. I started primary school in Istanbul, while my parents were away in the United States for a year doing research in education. My younger brother and I were looked after by my grandmother and aunt. My aunt was studying art and painting at the famous Academy of Fine Arts in Istanbul and she would sometimes take me along into her studio there, or let me sit in the canteen with other students. I was about five or six years old and, looking back, I realise how such an environment with so many young, passionate artists played an important role in my future life.

It was the era of Existentialism and Paul Sartre in Europe. I remember how all the art students would dress in black, and they wore French berets and small scarves around their necks. Most smoked cigarettes and talked about art and sculptures, paintings and philosophy.

I have no recollection of wanting to paint myself but remember being introduced to my aunt's tutor, Bedri Rahmi Eyupoglu, one of the early 1950s masters of Turkish Painting. I remember him towering over me and looking through some of my drawings, saying that I must also attend the Academy when I grow up! A few years ago, I was reminded by my deceased grandmother through another medium's communication that I used to do portraits as a child too! I had forgotten about the diaries my parents kept. They started these before our birth and continued until we were eighteen years old. They included the very first cuttings from our hair, traced outlines of our hands and feet for the first few months and years, along with their notes and reflections on how they felt towards us and each other. I was given my diary on my eighteenth birthday.

I remember starting to read them when my mother gave them to me but soon after I stopped. At the time, the diaries felt too personal and too melancholic. Now that I was reminded of their existence, I searched and found them. Yes, in one of my diaries there were several portraits, signed by me! I include a sample, below.

4- My drawings, at 5 years of age

My father noted under each drawing who they represented; grandfather, man from the side and Can, my brother, who was then three years old. He added under the last one that my brother was not happy with my drawing of him!

I remember having oil-painting classes at a very young age after my parents returned from the USA. My father was appointed president of a teachers' college in another city where I started a new primary school. Having spent so much time at the Academy of Fine Arts while so young, and being surrounded by young artists, I must have been impressed and possibly wanted to be an artist myself when I grew up! My parents always encouraged our interest in art and music. However, I do not know if it was my choice or my parents' idea. Like the piano lessons and ballet classes, my painting classes did not last long, and I had not done any serious paintings or drawings since I finished primary school.

Going through the diaries, I was also reminded about the drawings we did in primary school, although I no longer have them. We would be asked to illustrate celebrations like the National Day, showing the students' processions and street parties. I remember drawings lots of tiny people and patiently trying to fit them all onto the paper. I also recall trying to make sure that all their faces looked different from one another!

While still an architectural student, I was good at setting up perspectives and building models, but I never considered myself good at drawing or painting. Later, when I started working in an office, I would set up the views and then pass them on to someone else to make them look pretty!

In the early 1990s, in London, I had some free time on my hands as I was between jobs, and decided to return to oil painting. I still have the few small paintings I started but left unfinished. As an architect, I became accustomed to 'problem solving' but when it came to start a painting on an empty canvas, I was puzzled and found it frustrating. I did not know where to start. Now thinking about it, I believe it shows how restless my mind was at the time so my attempts to start painting again were not successful.

In 1994, I decided to accept a job offer in Brunei, Borneo, and I left London. It was the last time I attempted to paint until I moved back to the UK at the end of 1999.

31

4- FIRST STEPS

My first public demonstration was at an Open Platform I called my 'graduation platform' in the London Spiritual Mission on 25 July 2003. I had a link with a gentleman who lived in Scotland and was a dancer. At the time, Gordon Smith would demonstrate quite often at the London Spiritual Mission and was due to demonstrate the next day. He was well respected for both the accuracy and the manner in which he delivered his communications. At the time, I did not know that he had stepped into the church for a few minutes — exactly just before my demonstration. He accepted the communicator and the messages. I was over the moon!

Later in 2003, I began carrying a small drawing pad with me to the Spiritual Church services or any other demonstrations elsewhere. Very often I would be inspired to do a portrait or two while sitting and listening to the other mediums working on the platform. I would then offer them to the person who received a communication at the end of the evening. As far as I was concerned, it was a gift from the Spirit. Most of the time, they would recognise the person in the drawing, or sometimes, they would ask to take it to show it to other family members. On one occasion, after a demonstration at the Spiritualist Association of Great Britain (SAGB) in October 2003 when I gave a drawing to a young man who had received a communication earlier on, he said, "You gave me the shivers. This sketch may be of my uncle but I need to show it to my mother." Later I received the following message from him:

> *"Dear Esi, it was very nice meeting you last week at the demonstration at S.A.G.B. Thank you for the sketch of Richard. I discussed it with my mother who thinks it may well be her uncle. The few details you gave did fit quite well. Best wishes. Stephen"*

I still have the card. I kept it because it was one of the early positive feedbacks I received.

In 2003, Steve Lamont told me that I was ready for platform work but I did not have the courage to push myself. I started doing occasional demonstrations but also attended some of the three-monthly courses at the CPS to find out if short classes with different mediums, such as

Anthony Kesner, Ian Hunter and Angela Watkins would help me to develop further.

In 2004 I started taking classes at CPS. In the classes led by Ian Hunter, we used to sit quietly 'in the power' and it was the only additional class where I felt I was starting to get stronger links and clearer messages.

During the 'sitting in the power' part of one of his classes, I felt as if someone was touching me in the middle of my forehead. I later received the following message when back at home:

> *You wish to talk. I cannot give you unnecessary strength. Yesterday, you received healing from the hands put on you. Today, the energy I give is to increase your strength".*

> Me: "Who are you?"

> *"It is not important and it has no value to know who I am. The important thing is to increase your strength. It is not my duty but my aim to give you the strength which would show you your value"*

> Me: "Why?"

> *'We cannot polish you like a jewel yet. The power has to be used in order to be increased. It does not mean that so you can do what others can not. It means to stand and give messages that will convey hope and love flawlessly and easily".*

> Me: "Is it with Art or verbally?'"

> *"What you call Art is still a message, is it not? The importance is the message".*

> Me: "Who is helping me to do the drawings?"

> *"An artist from the beginning of the century, from the German school."*

A LESSON IN INTERPRETATION

One of my biggest lessons was given on an Open Platform for fledglings at SAGB. Steve Lamont, who was the leader of my development circle at the London Spiritual Mission, was now teaching at SAGB and was chairing the Open Platform. I arrived early at their magnificent building on Belgrave Square and sat in the sanctuary meditating before the start of the Open Platform. I was excited and scared! I knew that it would not be like any other fledgling platform because this time there would be a large number of the public and possibly some of the experienced mediums of SAGB.

As I sat in the sanctuary, I had the urge to draw the portrait of a gentleman. I then linked to a gentleman and sensed that he was the pilot of a war plane during World War II. I saw myself sitting in the cockpit of a jet plane and taking off to go to Europe. I also saw that a young woman with a little boy was standing outside, seeing him off. I knew it was a jet plane because the plane took off at a steep angle. As the plane climbed, I saw the young woman and the boy getting smaller and smaller. I knew that he left a young wife and a young son behind and that was his last memory of them. He was not coming back.

In the next visual image I was given, I was seeing him in the water. He was fully dressed with uniform and headgear, and there were a few others like him. All seemed to have fallen into the water and were sinking deeper and deeper. I then knew that he never made it back home.

Soon it was my turn. One of the rules of mediumship is to give the information as you receive it. It is never important for the medium to understand the 'what' or the 'how' of the story. Did I do that? No. Instead, I first held the drawing high for everyone to see and explained that he was a pilot, with a young wife and small son. I then said, "This man left for Europe in his jet but on his return it crashed into the sea!" Silence!

No one raised their hands or their voice. I turned to Steve, questioning what I ought to do. He replied, "Ask the gentleman who he is here for." I did, and he said that he is an uncle to someone in the room!

I repeated that aloud. I then followed it further with some other factual information he gave me about a lady who lives near the sea. He said that she has been decorating her home recently and he further provided us with some other detailed information. It was then that an elderly lady with white hair, sitting in the front, raised her hand and said he was her uncle.

What a relief it was! Later on, when I went over to give her the drawing, I asked why she had not responded earlier. She replied, "Well, you said his plane crashed into the sea, but what happened was that he was coming back on a ship, which was sunk"!

MY FIRST OFFICIAL DEMONSTRATION

There were a number of faces I regularly saw at the demonstrations and workshops held at SAGB, and in time we became friends, sharing our experiences with each other. In October 2004, Jeff Hewitt called with a problem: he was due to do his first official demonstration with two other new mediums from his class at SAGB but both, at the last minute, had to let him down. He asked if I would be interested in joining him as a spirit artist. I had just returned from Istanbul where I had given sittings and been doing workshops almost every night. Tired though I was, I nevertheless thought this would be interesting, almost like an understudy who goes on to become a famous performer after being given a chance to take somebody else's place!

The next day, we set off to a Jacobean mansion at Greenwich used as a community space. The demonstration was organised by Spiritual Links. The organiser was Katie, whose conversations seemed to be full of swear words! I met Jeff at Victoria Station and he drove us to the venue. There were more than a hundred people in the hall, all waiting for us! I did five sketches and three were recognised. One person was not certain and wanted to check with her mother so she took the fourth sketch. I was left with the last one, a sketch of a woman. The information I received was that her family were all fishermen but her husband worked with horses. I also saw her wearing riding trousers. The name I was given sounded something like Eleanor. No one claimed her, so I took the sketch home with me.

As far as the evening was concerned, we both thought that it had not been terribly successful as a first demonstration, but we also thought people were not being very responsive either. We said we must tell them to speak up next time! We thought we had made good links to the audience and to each other. However, as we were leaving, Katie said, "You must be grateful that people didn't walk out", which stunned us!

Six months later, I was in a workshop given by Gerry March at the College of Psychic Studies. The drawing I had taken home with me kept coming to my mind, and so I mentioned that I did Spirit drawings, and I told Gerry about the one that had never been claimed by anyone, repeating also, the information given to me. She said the information sounded familiar to her. Would I leave the portrait at the reception for her? Gerry called me the next day to say that she recognised the woman: her name is Elga. She said that Elga was one of her students and a friend from Stuttgart who had died two years earlier. Gerry was due to go to Germany the following day for her monthly classes and would take the drawing with her. She would give it to Elga's family. I was very happy to know that Elga found Gerry!

Jeff and I started working together. It takes a lot of courage to stand on a platform and deliver when you are new and on your own. I would start the drawing as Jeff linked to someone and give his evidence and messages. I would then finish the drawing and link to the person in the drawing. Sometimes it could be the same person we were linking to while at other times we had different links. Generally, it was expected that the psychic artist would only do the drawing and leave it to the other medium to provide the evidence and the messages. However, having been developed as a medium first, I could not help but link to the person as a mental medium when the drawing was completed. Jeff was comfortable with it once he realised that I was not trying to take over.

AUGUSTUS CAESAR

In October 2004, I travelled to Verona, Italy, with some friends for a long weekend. In the centre of the city are the ruins of a Roman arena dating back to the 1st Century AD, which used to hold up to 22,000 people. We visited the arena and saw that, inside, refurbishment works were being carried out and that the arena was divided into different sections.

The day we visited, a large number of these sections had tape around them, limiting access. The Royal Terrace was opposite the main entrance to the arena, and it was also cordoned off.

I was curious and wondered how it would feel to stand on that terrace, watching the events taking place in the arena. So, I am afraid, I ignored the tape and walked up to the terrace to stand and take in the whole view of the arena. As I walked towards the Terrace, one of my friends remarked, "Yes, go and see how it felt for Caesar!"

5- Photo of the Arena, Verona, Italy

Later in the evening we were at a restaurant and while waiting for our food to arrive I had the urge to do a drawing. I did not have my pad, so I started sketching on the heavy paper tablecloth. The first few lines drawn were some wavy lines and, thinking that it may be the beginning of a portrait, I asked for a piece of paper from the waitress and restarted the drawing. The drawing again started with the same wavy lines.

6- Augustus Caesar, Verona, Italy (Drawn 17.10.2004)

The portrait that appeared was of a man with wavy hair like that of Julius Caesar as he is represented in many sculptures! I heard him saying, "I was standing behind you on the Terrace, and now I am making myself known!" Who was this?, I wondered; was it possible that Caesar was communicating with me? I asked if he could give us some factual information. He said, "I had not been to the house of those noble classes in Verona, and I also did not know the meanness of those at the time, but I now know." He also said he is not buried with those nobles!

I was intrigued, but not able to do any research at the time. It was only while searching for a likeness of Julius Caesar for this book that I came across a photo of Augustus Caesar (his adopted son and heir) that showed an amazing resemblance to the portrait I had drawn all these years ago. So that's who it was!

During demonstrations, portraits would generally be drawn by starting with either the outline of the face or the eyebrow/s or the hairline, followed by the nose. However, as the evening goes on, I may find that the drawings start being sketched from different parts of the face. I feel that they do it so that I do not try to control the drawing, however unintentionally. It may then be the moustache or the mouth or reading glasses that appear first. In this case, it was the wavy lines that were difficult to relate to a portrait at first but in the end turned out to be the key to discovering the identity of Augustus Caesar.

THEY ARE READY WHEN WE ARE

I often used to go to Hampton Hill Spiritualist Church to experiment at their Open Platform, led by Sheila Thomas. It is a small Spiritualist Church in a purpose-built new building. There would usually be lots of new mediums, most with no previous platform experience, coming for the fledgling night to test their gifts. The fact that each of us was expected to give only one message made it much easier to stand on the platform.

One evening in November 2004, I planned to go to the Open Platform. In the morning, during my meditation, I asked my guides to help me to understand whether I am a spirit artist only or a mental medium as well.

We all did our demonstrations; I made two sketches, both of which were taken. After everyone took turns, Sheila announced that we had finished early and asked if anyone would be prepared to stand again. There was silence — nobody was volunteering but everyone was trying to shrink into their chairs. She turned to me and said, "You, would you like to come up again"?

I did not refuse but I was really worried as I walked up to the platform a second time. Usually, I would meditate at the beginning of the evening and would link with at least one spirit, and I would ask them to stay around until they had worked with me! Having done my demonstration earlier — and that one had gone well, I thought — I was suddenly scared that no one would be there to communicate with me!

As I ascended the platform and turned to face the crowd, it felt as if a miracle had happened! I felt as if someone had rushed into me with such force that my body was pushed forward. This time, I worked as a mental medium only. Not only was my question answered but, more importantly, I also realised that the Spirit would not disappoint us. They certainly would be there if we were ready and trusting.

THE NAME OF A CELEBRITY AS THE EVIDENCE

In March 2005, I was in Angela Watkins's class and I became friends with a lady called Melissa. At one of the classes, Melissa informed us that her 95-year-old mother had passed into spirit in Spain the day before. That evening in class, I recall immediately linking with a gentleman who was wearing a very smart suit and he told me that he had helped the lady in her passing. However, I did not have an opportunity to tell Melissa about it before the class ended.

After the class, some of us used to go to a bar for a drink. At the bar, I told her about this man and, by way of a brief description, I said he reminded me of David Niven, the famous actor. She gave me a big smile and said I could not have given her a clearer piece of evidence. Her father, who has been in spirit for some time, looked and moved like David Niven.

Melissa had a fond memory of her father she wanted to tell me. Her parents, she said, spent most of their time at their house in Spain and she very often travelled to Spain with them. She remembered once being at the airport with her father. She was only about eight years old and they were waiting to board their flight. She remembers her father talking to a man they had just met in the airport lounge. Her father was telling his new acquaintance what a wonderful daughter she was. That man was David Niven.

She also told me that in one of the earlier class exercises I gave her a warning about her mother's passing. I described her parents' house and said her father was in a smart black suit! Obviously, I was not aware of the significance of this message at the time.

THE FIRST PAID SERVICE

The first time we were paid for our demonstration was on 30 March 2005 at Richmond Spiritualist Church where we received £7.50 each! It was also the first time I had a direct link with my late father when I was meditating at home in preparation for the evening.

I was told by my guide that my father and my uncle would be with me that evening. He gave me the following message from my father:

> *"This is the beginning of successful work in the future. Do not worry. All in the congregation are waiting and are excited, all wishing links for themselves."*

Obviously, because I was not feeling terribly confident, I questioned. I asked if there was a chance that our future bookings may be in danger of cancellation, should we fail. He said:

> *"You must be joking! You will be smiling when you leave the church."*

On the way home, I was, indeed smiling as it turned out to be a successful demonstration. Later on, once at home, my father linked with me again to congratulate me!

That evening, after the demonstration, Jeff and I were given several bookings for the coming year.

In 2005, our names started appearing in *Two Worlds*, the monthly Spiritualist magazine established in 1887. Altogether we had five bookings for 2005, all at Richmond Spiritualist Church. We were so happy. Throughout my professional life, my having a very long and difficult foreign surname to pronounce made it challenging for most. I found out that people — from contractors on construction sites to clients in the various countries that I worked in — were happier to call me Architect Esi or Ms Esi.

Initially only my first name was used in the programmes of the Spiritualist Churches and the listings of the monthly *Two Worlds* magazine. However, because I worked together with Jeff and my first name was written before his, it appeared as if we were a couple.[3] Nothing wrong with that except Jeff is much younger than me and we were not a couple! I remember asking the churches to list his name before mine. My first name continued to be published in the advertisements until I was interviewed by *Two Worlds* in December 2010 as a working medium and artist. Thereafter, my surname would appear in the adverts in the magazine. I was touched that they took note except that now I had to explain to people that it was still me that was being advertised!

Working together with another medium had several additional advantages. Two mediums may have two communicators for the same person. At our second demonstration at Richmond Spiritualist Church, there was a small number of people in the congregation and all of my drawings were accepted. I remember that one of the portraits was accepted, though with some reservations, by a lady who was not completely sure that the sketch was of her sister because her hair looked different.

Jeff had a link with the sister. As I tried to link to my communicator, I was not listening to Jeff. I was seeing someone turning the pages of a newspaper and could hear the shuffling of the pages. I suggested that it might be the portrait of someone whose name or photo was in the papers. The lady said that the drawing should be of her aunt because her aunt had taken part in the Olympic Games and had won a medal. I suggested that they do some online research to see if they could find her name in one of the papers. So, she had messages both from her sister and aunt that day.

In another demonstration, I recall drawing the portrait of a gentleman. A lady in the room accepted it. I saw him in my mind's eye and knew that he kept walking in and out of the house. At first, I first could not make any sense of it. However, I then had a feeling that he was going out to a betting shop! At first I hesitated to tell her, but then decided that actually I had no option. It was the right choice: she gave a loud peal of laughter and said, "that's right, it is him!"

---

[3] "Esi and Jeff Hewitt" is how it appeared in print.

5- LESSONS FROM THE ESTABLISHMENT

I would visit SAGB often because they had excellent mediums demonstrating every day. After I had started doing portraits, I would quietly sit and watch the demonstrations and do sketches if I was inspired. Keith Hall was one of the mediums I respected. I went to one of his demonstrations in December 2004. After giving me good evidence and messages from my father and ex-mother in law, he asked whether I had already started doing public demonstrations. "You will be working from here soon," he added. "If not here, you will be doing public demonstrations. It is in your books. Just trust".

Ten days later, I went to see another good medium, Alan Acton, demonstrating. I was early, sitting and reading my book in the Conan Doyle Room where the demonstrations often took place, when Alan came in. We chatted for a while about SAGB and the CPS. We both thought of the CPS as being rather commercial and very busy, whereas SAGB, although it was the Spiritual Association, was all very quiet with only very few classes and workshops. Alan then left the room.

When he returned a little later, Alan asked if I would like to join him on the platform that afternoon! It was a great surprise and after "No, yes, no", I offered to do the sketches. After the first sketch, my pencil was jammed. After clearing the pencil, this time, the portrait did not work out properly. It was then I realised that the Spirit was telling me something: to work as a medium rather than do sketches. The energy was amazingly high and that's what I should have done. Standing next to Alan, I did not have the confidence yet, but I was over the moon with excitement. I thought Alan was such an angel. That is what I would expect SAGB to do for newcomers — encourage them and, as Alan does, take pride in doing so.

Earlier that day, on my way to the SAGB, I was told by my guides that I would return home very happy. I thought maybe that meant I would be given some encouraging messages. Yes, I was going back home very happy, as Keith Hall's prediction only ten days earlier — that I would stand and work at the SAGB — had been proved true!

On 18 February 2005, at another demonstration by Keith Hall, I was among the audience. I did two drawings and at the end of his demonstration, Keith kindly showed them to the people in the room. As I was talking to a lady who thought one of the drawings resembled her son, Keith called me to go over and have a look at a picture on a mobile phone held by a young man. The picture showed a man and a woman.

This young man had received a message from his mother earlier on. When I held the picture up for him to see, I also had to point out a strong jaw line for some reason I could not understand. The resemblance of my picture to the photograph on his phone was uncanny. He said the day his mother died she lost all her lower teeth and, maybe, that might explain the strong jaw line in the picture! I was again so happy!

In March 2005, I went to another Open Circle at the SAGB, chaired this time by Billy Cook, whom I admired as a medium. As usual, he started with a guided meditation and led us to a place with a beautiful light. He then left everyone alone to experience it for a few minutes. I felt I entered a very bright light. Two young girls of seven or eight years old came through. They were pulling me by the hand to go and play with them. Part of me left but part of me stayed because I had this very strong sense of pulsation in my forehead where the sixth chakra is said to be located. This was the very first time I had a clear 'sign', and it still is my 'sign', indicating when I am ready to communicate with the Spirit. At the end of the evening, when I mentioned it to Billy, he said that it is his 'sign' too.

I was happy with my development and all the support I received at SAGB, and also for being recognised as a developing sensitive by their famous mediums.

OUT ON MY OWN

It had been over a year since Steve Lamont said to me that I should start working on platform. I had gained some experience in the interim but was still delaying putting myself 'out there' with different churches. I kept joining different three-monthly development classes at the

44

CPS and doing other workshops. My excuse was to see how different mediums work with Spirit — in other words, how they receive and present information. But soon the time was to come that I would be able to be out, on my own — without always thinking I needed further lessons or the security of the "establishment". In retrospect, I can see that I was being given the help and encouragement I needed.

Meanwhile I completed my new flat and moved in. By word of mouth, I was now being invited to do some other refurbishment projects for others. Although such small architectural projects kept me going, they were not providing me with a steady income. I had tried to go through some employment agencies for Architects and Urban Designers some three years before; I had registered with two agencies but hadn't been called back. I had already given up finding a job through them when, out of blue, one of them telephoned me. It was in 2005 and they were inquiring if I would be interested doing some consultancy for English Partnership in Milton Keynes.

English Partnership was previously the Government's National Regeneration agency. Their aim was to set quality standards in urban design projects and the position required me to get involved in projects with Public/Private Sectors and Communities.

At that time, I had not worked on UK urban design projects for almost ten years. This offer of work made me so happy as it was the best I could have hoped for. Being offered a position where I would be overseeing current urban design projects meant not only that I could use my experience but also that I would gain the opportunity to reacquaint myself with the latest UK regulations and requirements. Besides, for an out-of-London office, to which I would need to commute daily, I was living in the best possible location. All I had to do was to take a train for two stops to Euston Station, then change for the Milton Keynes train on the other side of the same platform!

It was exciting to be involved in new projects and professionally stimulating — but travelling for three hours every day left me with no time for myself. After a year and a half, I started questioning whether I should be looking for another job, closer to home. And what happened? The other agency called and offered me a job in London!

During the time I was working in Milton Keynes, I could not afford to devote any time to any further development classes. At the same time, the numbers of Spiritualist Church services and demonstrations I was doing were increasing. I was being invited by different churches, and my experience and my trust in Spirit was growing.

LOST AND FOUND

Looking back, I can now appreciate how much I was being helped not only by the messages during our seances but also in the ways that I was encouraged to value my life — even though I sometimes had to be given 'lessons' before I took notice. I found an entry in my notes, which describes a busy Sunday in April 2006 when one of these amazing little lessons was given.

It seems that on that day I met a potential client for a refurbishment project in the West End of London. He was involved in converting a large space into a bar and wanted me to help with the interior finishes. The meeting and the site visit took most of my day. My notes say I then spent the rest of the afternoon in the shops, looking for a pair of trousers. And then, instead of relaxing and resting, I decided to go a large supermarket to do my weekly shopping.

First I went home to pick up my car. Arriving at the supermarket, I noticed that the parking area was full but I managed to find an empty space just opposite the main entrance.

I did my shopping, loaded the bags in the back of car, and drove home. It was then that I realised I did not have my shoulder bag with me. In my mind I began to reconstruct what might have happened. I had kept the keys to my car in my pocket along with the parking permit and placed the shoulder bag in the trolley, in front of me. I obviously paid for my shopping, which means that my bag was still with me. It would have been the last item remaining after loading the shopping into the car. I could not possibly have missed it. I checked the car but it was not there. Very annoyed with myself, I drove back to the supermarket.

All the way, I kept hearing that I would find it with everything safely inside. Still confused, I parked and walked back to the shop, first checking with Security at the entrance, and then with some of the staff members who were bringing back the trolleys left behind in the parking lot. None of them saw or found any bags. One of them suggested that I talk to the security manager inside, in case someone found and handed it to him. I went to the management office to enquire. No, no bags had been given in. However, the security manager then kindly offered to walk with me to where I had previously parked my car.

All this time, I was having a conversation with Spirit. They kept assuring me that it would be found and, increasingly annoyed, I kept saying stop fooling me by giving me false hope.

It was dark outside and I remember feeling really tired by this time. As we walked towards the place where my car had been, we both suddenly noticed something in the middle of the road, a little further away. As we approached, I realised it was my bag. Normally, one could have expected that with all the traffic, cars would have driven over it, and that staff taking the trolleys back to the shop would have seen it. I had also walked the same route when I came back to find the bag. But, there it was! I checked inside; nothing was missing. Most amazed, I thanked the manager and left the parking area with my bag. Driving back home, I inquired what happened: how could it possibly be? I heard the Spirit say, "Today you did not value your day. You did not think much about yourself, you kept pushing yourself to your limit for no good reason so we decided to make you run a bit more!"

Another lesson I received — in learning to trust and not worrying — came when I travelled to Istanbul to be with my mother for Christmas and the New Year holidays. Before my departure, a Russian colleague I was working with mentioned that her brother and his family were coming over to the UK, and would like to spend few days in London over Christmas. She was looking for a place for them to stay. So we agreed that I would leave my keys with her and they could stay at my flat.

Generally, I commuted to Milton Keynes by train, though sometimes I would choose to drive instead. During the journey, which normally took over an hour, I would listen to the radio. In the evenings, I would bring the radio back into my flat in its case. There is a stone shelf in my entrance lobby where I keep keys and notes for the day. I would also keep the radio case there to remind me to take it with me if I was driving anywhere else.

As I was getting the flat ready for the friend's family, I recall that I decided not to keep the radio in the lobby as no one would be using it and it would look tidier without it. So I stored it in an alternative place in the living room, in a box. I had my extra car keys with another friend who would keep an eye on my car, and start it and run it occasionally when I was away so the batteries would not be discharged in the cold.

In the new year, I arrived back home at the end of the week, giving me the weekend to get organised before returning to work. Everything in the flat looked as I had left it. I called my friend with whom I left my car keys, to report that I was back, only to be told off for leaving the car with the hand brake off!

On Sunday, I decided to go to a service at a Spiritualist Church. A friend of mine came to my place so we could drive there together. I checked the box where I'd placed the car radio case, but I could not see it there. I went downstairs and checked the car to make sure that I hadn't left it there after all, but it was nowhere to be found: not in the boot, not in the side pockets of the doors, nor the glove compartment. I even checked under the seats but could not find it. So we drove to the church without listening to the radio.

The next day, the first thing I did was check the car again for the radio. I could not find it. I could not decide whether to drive to Milton Keynes without the radio or take the train. As I was doing consultancy work, I wanted to make sure that I would have sufficient work for the week before purchasing a weekly train ticket. On the other hand, driving all the way to Milton Keynes without a radio would be boring.

As I was standing behind the car, trying to make up my mind, I kept hearing a voice telling me to take the car. It was getting louder and clearer, insisting that I should take the car. I could not understand why but finally I gave in. I opened the driver's door and sat inside. As

I looked down to my left, I saw it. I saw the radio! It was lying across on the hand brake (which I had engaged the previous night) and the passenger seat! At first, I could not believe my eyes, but then I started laughing. Because I also heard the voice saying "Would you now stop worrying about future work?" I smiled all the way to Milton Keynes, listening to Classic FM.

A LITTLE ENCOURAGEMENT

On my return from Istanbul, I was also feeling rather sad. My brother and I were best friends when we were young, but recently, I could not feel the same closeness and I was upset about it. I received the following advice soon after I came back from Istanbul, referring to my relationship with my brother.

> *"Relationships amongst siblings are difficult. Your thoughts are not much different but you have become 'strangers'. It is easy to re-establish friendship with him. You are sensitive. Sometimes to become friends you have to step on the pavement and give way."*

Followed by further advice:

> *"You do not fight anymore. When you are struggling with your thoughts, let it be. 'To know' is the main angst of humankind. They do not listen to their heart. We tell them not to fight, life is for living."*

It was very encouraging to be told that my attitude to life events was changing. I was now more willing to *accept* the challenges my life brought and not immediately try to control them. It was also a lesson on accepting people as they are and respecting their choices in their journeys, rather than trying to change them, for which I am now grateful.

PART 2

FACING THE PUBLIC

Demonstrating on the platform can be nerve-racking when one is just starting. In those early days, my way of calming myself, so I would not panic if I were unable to link to the Spirit, was to try to achieve the link before going out to the platform. I would sit quietly in the Medium's room and meditate until I felt the pulsation on my forehead, which would be my way of knowing that I was ready to work with the Spirit. I would then make sure to link with someone and ask them to stay with me!

I am always taught a lesson by Spirit at each demonstration. Having gone through a development and made aware of the different ways of receiving information from Spirit, it was now the time to trust that there would be a link.

Of course, it is most gratifying to be able to give accurate names, places, dates, etc., to recipients but this is not always possible. However, sometimes even a small piece of information I may consider too general turns out to have much meaning to the recipient. I recall communicating with an elderly lady at Burnt Oak Spiritualist Church, who said "my hand was held when I closed my eyes and found myself here" and then she went on to express her gratitude that her passing had been peaceful. As I repeated her words to the room, I was thinking "that is rather general — anyone could accept that."

In fact, though, the man who accepted the communicator later told me that she was his mother. She had been taken to a Swiss clinic for assisted dying. He sat next to his mother while she was given an injection; she simply closed her eyes and passed into spirit as he held her hand. He was grateful for being given not only strong evidence but also comforting news from his mother. That was another lesson for me. It showed me that even simple words or acts can mean a lot to someone. If the Spirit gave that information, I should trust and deliver.

The Spirit, however, also expects me to keep doing regular meditations, especially before any services or demonstrations, and not to rely on them only. I always feel that my energy is not 'lively' enough — either for sketching the drawings or receiving information from Spirit — if I have not meditated beforehand. Once I was told after such a demonstration that "personalities were correct but your energy did not pick up all that was given easily. Accept the fact that you should do your bit first and then expect us to bring the evidence." They added "you simply open the door of your home and invite us in. We come in, see you and talk to you. Just feel at home."

6- SOME INTRIGUING COMMUNICATIONS

During the early Open Platform demonstrations, I worked only with my mediumistic gifts — hearing, sensing, seeing, and feeling. As my mediumship developed, so too did the spirit portraits. I would then include portrait sketching in my demonstrations, as for me they are hard evidence that life is eternal. I have done hundreds of portraits, which I give away, and some kind people return copies of the drawings to me along with a photograph with which they found a resemblance. Some are willing to share these photographs together with details such as names, dates, etc., while sometimes they ask me to use only the initials of the person in the portrait, a request I always honour.

It is, however, understandable that it is not always the case that people send me copies of my sketches or photographs of the people I have drawn.

Below are some of the stories of communications without portraits, and others which, although I did do portraits, these were taken away and I was not subsequently given copies or photographs.

THE IMPATIENT LADY

As I got used to giving demonstrations, my confidence that the Spirit would work with me grew and I stopped trying to link in advance. Now, I simply trust that someone will link when I am ready, but one evening I did not expect to have two communicators arriving at the same time, one of which turned out to be a very impatient communicator!

It happened at a demonstration at Clapham Spiritualist Church; I felt two communicators arriving almost simultaneously. I had to go ahead with one of them, and asked the other one to hang on quietly. Having communicated with the recipient of the first link and given their messages, I was finishing when I felt a sharp pain on my leg. Looking down, I could not believe my eyes. I 'saw' in my mind's eye that the second communicator was a small elderly lady with a walking stick who, growing impatient, was poking my leg with her stick!

A LITTLE ANGEL

I very often find my communicators are children in spirit. This time, it was at an Open Platform at Barnes Healing Church. It was my turn to do the mental mediumship and as I stood there, anxious to link, I became aware of a little girl and 'saw' her in my mind's eye. She appeared to be about four or five years old, happily swimming in a pool and wearing a blue swimming costume. Without warning she became motionless and I realised she was telling me that she had drowned.

It is always very difficult to inform an audience that the communicator is a child and to describe how the small child died. So, I chose to spare them the details and just say that I was linking to a little child who tragically lost her life. There was a lady in the back and a young couple sitting near the front row who all raised their hands. When I mentioned that it was a little girl that I was seeing, only the young couple signalled to continue. They then accepted the description I had given. They had tears in their eyes.

The little girl that I was seeing was now very active, full of joy, jumping all around and laughing. She said "I am a little angel now. When I grow up, I will be a big angel". Tragic as it was, it was also lovely to see her happy, healthy and laughing, dancing around. I hoped that it gave her parents some comfort.

A MESSAGE I COULD NOT GIVE

I usually arrive at the church about 45 minutes before the service starts so that I can set up my easel, and then have enough time to sit quietly and meditate for a while. On this occasion, I was again to work with Jeff Hewitt at Wimbledon Spiritualist Church.

At the time, I would start sketching a portrait and tune in to the communicator after the drawing was completed and then give verbal information to a potential recipient. Sometimes, Jeff would tune in to the person in the drawing and give further evidential information to the same recipient. However, occasionally, we would work independently, linking to different communicators. As time passed, we found we were able to receive more and more information and eventually we decided to work independently, which is what we were doing on this particular day.

I was early and still setting up the easel when a young man arrived in the church hall. He was early too. We greeted each other. He was friendly and gave me a big smile. Later, during the service, one of the portraits turned out to be of his grandfather. He accepted both the drawing and the description of the person I had given verbally.

The grandfather then mentioned that there were plans for a wedding, which I repeated to him. The young man very cheerfully accepted and said, "Yes, I am getting married." As I opened my mouth to pass on the next message I expected to receive, the grandfather said, "No, he won't." Astounded, I just froze with my mouth open!

I quickly managed to regain my composure outwardly, but was struggling desperately to find a way of putting it to him. Normally I would not have hesitated to pass the message on, but I simply was not prepared for anything like this, and did not know what to say next! It was funny, but at the same time it was not. I was so surprised that I could not even try to make it sound like a joke! Luckily, his grandfather came back with his next message and said "everything will be fine" which I then delivered.

I never found out what happened. The young man happily took the drawing before he left.

SHE HEARD HER FATHER'S WISH

Once, I was at a lecture given by a well-known and respected medium. A woman raised a question: whether stillborn children would have spirits. She had been told that the spirit chooses the person at the moment of conception. It made me wonder at the time, as I had no knowledge of such details, and remained unsure. However, I believe I found the answer some time later, when I did a demonstration at Clapham Spiritualist Church in 2009.

I did the portrait of a young woman who appeared to be around the age of nineteen. She had long straight hair and was wearing a garland of fresh flowers on her head. I usually pick up the character of the person communicating first as the unique traits of character are easier to recognise by the recipients. However, this time, it was proving difficult — I could not feel what kind of person she was, or pick up on her mannerisms or any other features that makes us who we are. All I felt was that she was a lovely person.

A woman sitting on her own was hesitant but said, "I have a daughter and she looks like her sister." I was given a name, so I asked, "Who is Sophie?" She replied, "Her name was Sofia." I said, "She tells me that her hand never touched the earth?" The woman answered, "Yes, she was stillborn."

I then gave her the message from her daughter to the family. She later came to collect the portrait and said Sofia would have been nineteen years old. Also, interestingly, that same evening, her husband told her that he would not be coming to the church with her but that she would come back with a drawing! Obviously, the daughter heard her father's wish!

Communicating with a stillborn child is not only a sensitive issue but also a difficult one. I was happy that she provided her parents with a drawing of herself and remembered her name.

HE WAS BEING HERSELF

In September 2009, I was doing a Sunday Service at Hampton Hill Spiritualist Church. My last drawing was of a woman and the information I was receiving was related to an elderly lady. However, each time I looked at the drawing I also saw a man. Initially nobody claimed the drawing. I then asked if anyone would know a man who liked dressing as a woman. Three people came forward and, after I gave further descriptions of the communicator's personality and his extensive travels through Europe, one of the three was identified as the recipient.

I then asked the communicator why he came through as a woman — as the recipient did not seem to have much familiarity with his experiences as a woman. He answered that he came through in that way because it was the first time he was being himself. He thanked the recipient and asked everyone not to be judgemental of others, to accept each person as they are, and share what they have to offer. I thought it was a really good ending to the evening.

THE PORTRAIT OF THE SON

Another first was at the Barnes Healing Church in June 2010. As part of the evidence, I am sometimes given visual images of past memories that had been shared by the recipient and the person in spirit. These images may be part of a scene or an event represented by a picture or I see them as if watching part of a film. I then share it with the person in the room.

Occasionally, the recipient is one of the role players in the scene! To me, it is sometimes clear especially if I can recognise the recipient who is sitting across from me. However, when the events being portrayed had taken place years earlier, when everyone looked younger, it may not be as easy to identify immediately if those I am seeing are alive or in spirit at the time.

That evening, one of the portraits drawn was of a young boy about ten years of age. I could see a young lady standing behind the young boy and feeling very proud; I could also sense that she was his mother. After I passed on the information, a gentleman sitting in the back raised his hand and said he is the boy in the portrait.

The resemblance to him, even though he was now much older, was striking. He then explained to us that the drawing showed him at the age he was when he lost his mother. It was very touching to realise that his mother chose to have her son's portrait drawn rather than her own at an age when they were last together!

7 - PORTRAITS AS EVIDENCE

With my new emerging gift for drawing portraits, I decided to go to a workshop to sharpen my skills in portraiture. I attended only one class at SAGB given by Bill Forester. In the class, we were shown the standard relative proportions of the facial features such as eyes, ears, mouth, and so on, and how these features relate to each other. We were encouraged to first sketch a set up — with few simple lines to mark where the features should go — before starting on a portrait.

Encouraged by this information, I started experimenting with very faint pencil lines, putting this preliminary diagram down on the paper first and then starting the portrait. That way, I felt more confident, thinking that this would allow the face on the paper to be three dimensional — in other words, more realistic!

Later on, I thought it might be a good idea to buy some books to gain some formal knowledge myself about the bone and muscle structures of the human face. I had found most of the drawings by some of the other psychic artists rather 'naive' with features appearing flat, and a sort of sameness to them all. Having purchased two books, I came home, all excited, and sat down to read and sketch. After about an hour, following the instructions in these books, I had to stop to attend to something else. Later in the evening, I had a strong urge to do a portrait, which I include below.

7- Portrait of an unknown man

It was so very quickly done that I did not have the time to think about what I was doing and where the guiding pencil lines should go! It turned out to be a lovely drawing of a man whose facial proportions did not need to have been fitted around a preparatory setup as I'd been taught. I never found out who he was but he helped me to learn a more important lesson: I was being told that "it is not you doing the drawings." So, I put the books aside, never to open them again!

I continued going to the demonstrations and sketching when inspired. I would give the pictures to people as a gift from the Spirit. Some would say they could recognise the face, and that was enough to make me happy. But then I had my very first 'evidence'!

THE FIRST DRAWING AS EVIDENCE

8- W.S., 1900- 1956 (Drawn 9.2.2004)

This portrait was the very first in response to which I received a photograph from the recipient of a portrait drawing. The recipient was a lady in an advanced development class at the College of Psychic Studies in February 2004. Even though I was told by my Closed Circle leader that I was ready to start to work as a medium, I was reluctant. First, I did not know where to start. Would I visit churches and offer to work during their services? Would they give me an opportunity? But I did not have the confidence even to do that. Yes, I could do one or two communications at a time, but working as a medium would require standing in front of people and delivering communications for at least 45 minutes. Instead, I decided to join different short classes for a while and see if I could learn anything else from them.

The College of Psychic Studies did not have development circles but offered weekly classes for three months at a time. I joined the one run by Anthony Kesner. It was an advanced class, which advertised that the group would also be taken to churches to practise. It was exactly what I thought I needed, however it did not turn out as I expected. So I left after several months; nevertheless, some good came of it as I had my very first evidence, which gave me the boost of confidence I needed!

In the class, we would be asked to do different exercises, for example some would entail each medium giving individual communications to someone in the group, or there could be smaller group exercises in which two or three people would form a group and take turns to communicate for the others.

One day, we were asked to form pairs, sit face to face, and take turns to communicate with someone in spirit for each other. We would give evidential information about that person first and then pass on their messages.

I was working with one of the women in the group as I linked to a gentleman. As I was giving information about him, I also had the urge to do a drawing. So I offered to do it for her. As we were told not to 'feed' information to each other during the exercise, she did not tell me whom the drawing belonged to. It was the portrait of a man. She seemed to recognise the drawing and said she also accepted the information given about the person. I gave the drawing to her and we continued with her doing communication for me.

The following week she came back with a picture of her parents. It was the first time someone gave me feedback for my drawing and I could not believe my eyes. I was speechless!

DRAWING OF A PERSON STILL ALIVE

This sketch shows the very first portrait I drew of a person who was still alive when it was drawn. I was again in Istanbul, visiting my mother. I'd met a friend for the afternoon and on returning home had a strong feeling that I should do a sketch. I sensed that it could be related to this friend. Earlier, she mentioned that her brother had recently passed into spirit. I had never met him, nor did I know anything about him, so I wondered if it was his portrait that I sketched. When I called and told her about the drawing, she responded with excitement and was interested to see it.

9- Kemal G. 1926- 2005 (Drawn 28.12.2004)

She invited me for dinner the next evening and suggested that she would also invite her brother's family so they could all meet me. As planned, I went to her place, met the family, and put the drawing on the table for all to see. My friend's husband could not join us as he was ill, in bed, and under medication, so was unable to view the drawing.

All the family gathered around the table, looking very curious. They looked at the drawing, then at each other with questioning expressions on their faces, all the while whispering to each other. From their reactions, I simply assumed that they did not recognise the person or were not sure, and that they were trying to be polite. My friend said she would like to show it to her husband later when he awakened. I again assumed that my friend, too, was being polite, and did not want to disappoint me. So I left the drawing with them.

The next morning, she called and confirmed that the drawing had a strong resemblance to her husband's stepfather. However, she pointed out, he was still alive! At the moment I was drawing his portrait, he was at the hospital having a blood transfusion. She told me that they would check to see if there were any photographs of him, and they later emailed me the drawing and the photograph above. I was astounded. It was the first time I had done the portrait of a person who was alive! At the time, I did not know why. It was some time before I found out!

THE TRUE EVIDENCE

Some close friends of mine, who were an architect couple living, and running their own practice, in London, always tried to keep anything to do with the Spirit at arm's length. In 2005, while I was doing my spiritual development, the husband was undergoing kidney dialysis. Later on, we found out that he was also suffering from cancer. Throughout my development, I used every opportunity to share my experiences of spirit communication with them by giving them my latest stories.

My so-called reason for telling them was simply to share my fascination with the incredible concept that there is no death — however difficult it was for them to accept. In fact, I wanted to show them that my most incredible experiences indeed *proved* that I could communicate with our loved ones in spirit. I thought that if I could illustrate to them that there is no death as such, it might give them the strength to face the illness with more courage. I could tell they found my stories fascinating as well but somehow they did not want to take them seriously.

She and her husband would listen to my stories but at the end of each story, she would say, "Come on Esi…!" I persevered, however, telling them my stories whenever I visited. While they smiled and listened politely to me, I could tell that they did not take it seriously. But then it happened that she was able to witness for herself something of what I had been telling her about over time. She wrote about the event, and I quote her account below:

10- M. Muhtar H. 1894- 1981 (Drawn 3.4.2005)

While I recognise and value the spiritual aspect of our existence as human beings, and although I have always accepted that there are phenomena that science can not explain, I have never been enthusiastic about "communicating with spirits". However, I am still in awe over the following events.

"Once we were in the company of a friend of mine, when Esi said she was receiving a message for me. The message turned out to be from my deceased father, with loving and heart warming words. At the same time she started drawing the portrait of a man who in some ways did look like my father, but the bow tie was so uncharacteristic. The most formal dress he wore, as far as I could remember, was a suit with a tie. 'If he were to

present himself in the most recognisable way, he should have worn something on his head — his French style beret outside, or a cap at home — which he took to wearing as his hair was thinning out in his old age!' I said.

"A few months later, when my friend visited my sister at our family home, my sister showed her my parents' wedding photograph, which I had long forgotten about. There was my dad wearing a bow tie!"

"B. B. London, UK (Feb. 28, 2010)"

TOLD HOW TO LOCATE PHOTOGRAPH

The second time I was given a portrait that belonged to a person still alive is shown below. Again, I did the drawing while I was sitting at home on my own. The drawing was made in December 2004 and I did not know to whom it belonged. I was not given any clues either. In June 2005, I was going through the drawings I kept at home and I came across it.

As I sat thinking who she could be, I received a message. I was asked to contact the same friend whose father's portrait I had previously drawn. I was told to call and ask my friend to take out her old picture album, which included photographs taken at her and her husband's engagement party.

I called and informed her. I then took the drawing to my friend, showed it to her, and gave her the message. She looked at it but was hesitant to say who the person could be. She took out the photos of her engagement party, which was held in 1972.

11- H. Nevher B. 1911-2006 (Drawn 6.12.2004)

It was only when we went through her old photos together and found the one above, that she had to admit that the drawing was of her mother-in-law. We were both amazed. At the time, she was still alive but she was suffering from Alzheimers. Unfortunately, I again was not aware that the drawing of her indicated that she was being sent healing by someone in spirit until quite a few years later. How I found out is described in *Part 3, Section 13 - Confirmation of Healing Sent*, when the communicator told us loud and clear! Had I known this at the time, I'd have tuned into the Spirit once more to find out the identity of the communicator who was sending her healing. It could well be that the communicator was her son, my friend's late husband.

As my friend, still in mourning for her late husband, was not willing to get involved in spirit communication, I did not enquire further.

How fascinating it was that I did the drawing some six months earlier and had to wait till much later to find its owner. Maybe it was hoped that with the passing of time, my friend would be more open to the idea of spirit communication!

AN APOLOGY

The story below was most amazing. I met this lady for the first time at a friend's house. She was in the UK to visit her daughter and, for the next few days, she would be staying with my friend in London. As we were sitting and having tea, it was mentioned to her that I communicate with the Spirit and am guided to do Spirit drawings. She seemed interested, and so I offered to do one for her.

I knew nothing about her. Once again I am going to allow her to tell the story, which I quote from a letter she later sent.

12- Sevket K., 1911- 1992 (Drawn 3.4.2009)

"In our world with hardened materialistic values, whenever I want to incite some spiritual awareness to the people around me, I tell them the story of my experience with Esi.

"I met Esi several years ago through a mutual friend. She knew nothing about my life and a few hours after we met, she offered to make a drawing for me. The drawing that she did, and the message she conveyed, which was given in a shy, hesitant, reluctant manner were most amazing. The outcome was a portrait of my father in his youth.

"At that time, I was in my late 50s and had almost no contact with my father all through my life. He had been away from me when I was a small child and I only met him few times when I was in my 20s and 30s. I hardly had any conversation with him during his life, and had never seen him as in the drawing. But, in my album, I had a small photo of him, almost exactly like what Esi drew.

"Since Esi lives in the UK and I in Turkey, we don't meet often. During our next meeting, a social gathering with lots of people, Esi felt some soul was trying to communicate with her and related this to me. This time a loving aunt had contacted, just to say 'hello' to me".

—*Mine K. 26.2 2010*

HOW WE REMEMBER THEM

One of my dearest and oldest friends in the UK is someone with whom I shared a house when I was studying in Oxford. She still lives in Oxford and is now a professor at the University. I do not see her and her husband as often as I would like to, but we keep in contact by occasionally visiting each other and by calling every Sunday for a chat.

They were also following my spiritual development with curiosity. On one of my weekend visits, I offered to communicate with someone for them. Just before I left for London, we decided that I would do a sitting for her husband.

He sat across from me while I was sketching on a pad placed on my lap. As I did the portrait, I also passed on to him the verbal information I received. I was describing the person both in physical appearance and personality, also giving their memories, as they were conveyed to me. He could not see the drawing clearly but he kept saying "Yes, that is my father, yes, yes …" confirming that he accepted the information as correct.

13- Willie W. 1896- 1984 (Drawn 13.3.2005)

It was only when I showed him the drawing that he hesitated, and said he was now not so sure! We left it there and I asked him whether he would check the photographs he had of his father to see if that might help.

I returned to London and later that evening received his email to which was attached a photograph of him with his father, taken some years earlier, along with a copy of the portrait. Referring to the drawing, he wrote, "You know, that is not how I remembered him."

It is, of course, true. We do not always remember people as in photographs. We remember them by the tone of their voices, their manner of speaking, the words they use, their smile, the way they laughed or even smelled. Yes, the photo he sent me shows his father wearing his glasses, whereas the portrait does not. However, other than that there is an undeniable resemblance. I believe he felt the same!

HE CAME TO SAY GOODBYE

In November 2005, I was at a seminar in London given by the well-known and respected spiritual medium, Gordon Smith. There were a number of people sitting in the row in front of me. One of the girls volunteered to stand and experiment with her gifts.

During her demonstration, I had the urge to do a sketch and felt that it was related to her. It was a portrait of an elderly gentleman. I could also see him in my mind's eye. He had a beautiful smile on his face and his eyes were shining with joy. Later on, I showed the portrait to this lady. She smiled, reached for her handbag and came back with a photograph. In the picture, there was a man and a woman.

She said they were her aunt and uncle. In fact, she said, at that moment, he was in a coma, at a hospital in the USA.

14- F.W., 1928- 2005 (Drawn 27.11.2005)

I was intrigued because I had no idea if the spirit of someone in a coma could contact me. We exchanged email addresses and she promised to send me the copies of both for my portfolio, which she did, a few days later. However, her email also contained the news that her uncle passed into spirit around 3.30pm on the Sunday before, while we were at the seminar. In fact, he had come to say goodbye to her!

THE GRANDMOTHER

There are no Spiritualist churches in Istanbul. To my knowledge, the possibility of continuation of life after death is not a concept people are readily familiar with. As in other parts of the world, there are many psychic mediums, as people like to be told their fortunes. The most popular form of psychic mediumship is the reading of Turkish coffee cups. In fact, everybody loves Turkish coffee and there are always a few people in every family who are good at 'reading' coffee cups.

In the early 2000s, my spiritual development in London was followed with curiosity by my friends in Istanbul and it seemed the word of my activities soon spread. Each time I went back to be with my mother, there would be requests from friends of friends, who wanted to meet me and to witness a spirit communication!

I was only too happy to oblige as it meant I could practise. Although it was a completely foreign experience for them, they nevertheless were willing to try! I could not only provide them with evidential information about their loved ones in spirit but also draw portraits of them. Working in Turkey gave me the advantage of communicating in my mother tongue, which meant that in addition to the natural ease of speaking in one's first language, even more importantly, while passing on their information and messages, I could mimic their manner of speaking and the words, even the dialects, as the letter below demonstrates.

The portrait below was drawn at a meeting in Istanbul. Not only did the photograph show a great resemblance to the portrait I had drawn, but also the conversation provided the further evidence. I include the letter I received from the recipient below.

15- Zahide E. 1900- 1989 (Drawn 2005)

"I had a few sittings with Esi and in most of them my grandmother was the person who communicated. I immediately recognised the portrait when it was drawn. Later I could find only one photograph of her and the resemblance was striking. The interesting thing was the manner of her talking, her accent and the words she used. There is no one else in the family who uses these words. Such strong evidence was given that I now believe in the afterlife without a shadow of any doubt. Each time we had a sitting my conviction only became stronger.

"Erendiz T., İstanbul (June 6, 2010)"

8- HELPING HAND FROM A MASTER ARTIST

As the number of spirit portraits I did increased, I noticed that I started working with more than one spirit artist. Not only did the styles of the drawings vary, but also the energies working with me felt different. I could not claim to be producing any art of great value in terms of line drawings but that was not my concern at all. In fact, I found it amazing that they could produce such excellent drawings, showing character and expression but in addition with so much resemblance to the person. This was more than enough for me!

In my view, these drawings were produced in spite of me as I was not someone trained as an artist. I believe that what may have helped was that, in my professional life as an architect, I did feel comfortable working with a pencil and I have always had a sense of proportion. But that was about it! To this day, I do not know the names of the artists working with me although I feel different pencils are used by different artists. There is only one exception to that, which I was made to discover while at an exhibition!

HENRI MATISSE

I would often take the bus that runs alongside the Victoria and Albert Museum in South Kensington on my way to classes at the College of Psychic Studies. I kept promising myself to visit the museum soon as it had been a long time since I was there last. One Saturday, in March 2005, I decided just to do that. As I was getting ready to leave, I also remembered that I had seen an advertisement for the *Matisse: His Art and His Textiles* exhibition at the Royal Academy of Arts at Piccadilly the day before. It suddenly felt very tempting to visit both so I decided to go to the Royal Academy first as it would be on my way to the Victoria and Albert Museum.

As I walked into the courtyard off Piccadilly, I saw a very long queue of people waiting to go into the exhibition. Not wanting to wait, I decided to come back later or even another day. I crossed the street and took the next bus to the Victoria and Albert Museum. However,

I heard a voice saying "No, leave the bus and go back." I ignored it at first, but it grew louder and more insistent. Finally, I had to go along with it and got off the bus after two stops. I walked back, dreading the long queue. To my surprise, the courtyard was almost empty!

The exhibition was on the upper floor, occupying only a few rooms. Matisse's paintings along with the textiles he used in his paintings were being displayed. I was enjoying it more than I expected. It felt as if I was being filled in with colour with each painting. It was a delightful exhibition. In the last room, there was a smaller collection of his pencil drawings. As I turned the corner I found myself facing these smaller drawings. I had to stop as I was taken aback. Thoughts raced through my mind as I remembered a number of portraits drawn only a week before that were executed in a similar style: "Could it be? No, how could it be? But, it does... No, of course not, who do you think you are?"

I was struggling to accept this as I recalled some of the recent portraits I had sketched shortly before the exhibition. Unfortunately, I do not have copies of these to include here as I gave them away to various recipients who had claimed them. These portraits were drawn in strong outlines with limited details. At the time, I remember thinking to myself that they reminded me of Matisse drawings, but of course, not taking it seriously. But now, standing in front of his drawings, I experienced a mixture of feelings: elevated, confused, almost scared!

I thought I should go out, have lunch, and come back again. I had to go through the whole of the exhibition and also try to think why I was feeling rather confused looking at his pencil drawings. At the exit, I was told that I would not be allowed in again should I leave as this was a popular show, and the crowds were larger than expected. Not wanting to leave without going through exhibition again, I decided to go around once more, and ended up walking through all of the rooms three more times, making me feel virtually filled up with great joy. Finally I left the exhibition, and took the bus with the intention of going to the Victoria and Albert Museum next to have my lunch there.

The bus was full and I squeezed myself into a corner. I started feeling the urge to do some sketches and it was getting stronger and stronger inside me. I found a piece of paper and a pencil in my bag, and started sketching. With the bus moving, it was rather difficult to sketch standing up but I ended up doing the two sketches below.

16- Two sketches (Drawn 25.3.2005)

Whenever I finish a portrait, I always sign it with my name and the date in the corner. This was never the result of a conscious decision; in fact those elements have always been like part of the drawing itself and done automatically — just as putting a dot at the end of a sentence is. This time, written next to my name was Matisse!

In the following days, there were a number of continuous line drawings similar in boldness and simplicity. I include two of them below. I cannot recall where they were drawn and it seems they were not claimed as I could find no photographs with any resemblance. Both of the sketches were different and this time signed Esi + M.

17- Two unknown portraits (Drawn 27.3.2006 and 2.7.2005)

9 - PORTRAITS BY SPIRIT

Soon I was receiving more and more photographs of the people I sketched. I consider the portraits not only as gifts from the Spirit but also as hard evidence that life continues after death. It is such evidence that even those who take a cynical stand on life after death, and argue that what all the mediums do is only 'cold reading', cannot explain or justify. After all, the portrait is the drawing of someone I have never met before in my life, and as illustrated in the previous chapters, people do not necessarily carry the memories of their family members in their mind as images. In addition, the portraits may be of people no one in the room met before, yet they would find their way to the right owners. More about that in *10- You as the Messenger.*

Mediums who draw portraits are usually termed 'Psychic Artists'. I do not feel that this title applies in my case. First, I am not the artist because I am not sketching anyone whom I see as I do the drawing. Second, I do not 'pick up' the information in the form of pictures from the sitters' energy as Psychic Mediums may be able to do when they do 'readings'.

I have heard of some mediums who say they see the person in spirit first, and then sketch their portraits. I also hear that there are some courses that teach how to draw the features of the face — lips, eyes, eyebrows, etc. I feel that mediums working this way may earn the title 'Psychic Artist' because they are the ones doing the sketches rather than the Spirit. In my case, however, I feel the term 'Spirit Artist' does more justice to what I do and describes it more accurately.

I include further examples to illustrate that Spirit uses the portraits not only as 'evidence' of the continuation of life in spirit, but also as an additional tool to reach a wider number of people and for different reasons. This can be challenging as well as exciting to facilitate, and is also discussed further in *10- You as the Messenger.*

At the start of a service or demonstration, I give a brief explanation about how Spirit works with me and what to expect, or even what not to expect!

The first thing I emphasise to an audience is that they should have an open mind as each demonstration is not only unique, but also an experiment. All I am doing is allowing myself to be used as an instrument by which Spirit can communicate; I do not know who is around, neither do I choose who should come through or what they should talk about. I am just the medium in between our material world and theirs, and it is a privilege I do not take lightly. Generally, the following is what I tell them about the demonstration itself.

The process is not like that of a portraitist who looks at their subject and sketches — because I do not see anyone while I am drawing. To me it feels as if someone enters into me and guides my hand. I am as curious as anyone else watching to see who is going to appear on the paper.

To start with, I do not know if it is going to be the portrait of a male or a female, an old or a young person. It is only after the face appears on the paper that the energies I work with change, and only then will I link to the person in the drawing as a mental medium.

I know that there are different artists working through me at each demonstration. During the demonstration, the styles of drawings and the energies that I work with may change. For example, while some artists work with short broken lines and use shadows, others draw with very simple and continuous lines. Their energies are also reflected in the way my arm moves: some movements are more energetic than others. Regardless of who the artist is, the drawings are usually completed within two to three minutes.

The energies I work with will change once the drawing is completed and I will work as a medium; I may hear, see or feel them. I would then pass on this information verbally and I emphasise to the people in the room that they should respond to me in a loud and clear voice. The reason is that it is their voice that carries their energy to the spirit. My feeling is: no voice, no easy recognition!

This reminds me of an old Doris Day film! In it, the father calls home and his little son answers. The father inquires if the mother is at home. In fact, she is in the bath tub, which is why she did not answer the call herself. The little boy nods his head in reply, but of course the father does not receive any response, so he asks again. And again the boy nods! This goes on for a while, to the total frustration of the father!

I was young when I saw this film and it stuck in my mind because it made me laugh. I now tell people that their loved ones would feel equally frustrated if the person answering their call keeps nodding their head (or speaks softly)!

Next, I tell them that they should not feed me information about the person in spirit. It is important that they should acknowledge by simply saying 'yes', 'no', or even 'possibly'. I do not need to know the details as long as the recipient can accept what is given to them; all I am doing is putting my mind aside and simply passing on the information I receive. Any details given may encourage me to start interpreting, and even try to meet their expectations, while all I should do is be the medium between the two worlds.

Another point I raise before the demonstration is that the portraits are not photographs, only sketches. The drawing may show the person when they were younger or as they looked when the recipient last saw them before their passing into spirit. More often than not, the person appears as they do in the drawing because there is a photograph somewhere with great resemblance.

On my part, there is always this feeling of anticipation when I turn around to face the people watching, expecting and hoping that someone will recognise the person. Many times they do. They raise their hand and say that they think they know the person. Other times, of course, this doesn't happen, and then I link to the person in the drawing to give us further information so they can be identified more easily.

Once I link to the communicator, the first thing I feel is their personality. I then describe how I feel; I may feel like someone who is an optimist, carefree and light, or possibly I feel like a sombre person. I may again feel or even see their physical characteristics and what they look like: slim, upright, someone who used to drag their feet while walking, etc. Or they may show me the environment around them if it is part of their shared memories; if it is a flat or a house, the layout, the furniture, the kitchen or paintings on the walls, etc. I may even pick up an aroma or scent if that is what they think would help to be identified with — for example the smell of someone who used to smoke cigarettes, or somebody's perfume. That is the information I would give to the potential recipients verbally. Such additional information would, of course, make the recipients feel assured that it is the correct person even after the person in the portrait has already been recognised.

The responses to drawings are so different. While some are amazed by the details given in the drawing (such as a dimple on a chin or the type of necklace or hat they are wearing), some others hesitate because it would not be exactly the hairstyle they wore or even how they remembered their relatives. As I've said before, it is not often that people are remembered as in pictures — many other characteristics play a part — but I am certain there is a reason why they choose to have the portraits drawn as shown.

I usually bring a photo album with me to the demonstrations. In the album, I have copies of individual drawings along with the photographs that the recipients sent me afterwards. For me, putting them together is the simplest way of illustrating the resemblance between the drawings and the photographs.

I also find that it is important to have them with me for another reason: there are usually newcomers who have not seen portraits like this done before. In fact, some might even be new to the idea that life is eternal and that we can communicate with those who have passed into spirit.

The portraits and photographs may show different degrees of resemblance between them but they definitely illustrate that it is not possible to confuse the people with each other. I have not yet encountered anyone who could argue that the features of the drawings are all the same or suggest that any one portrait might belong to another person in another photograph.

I like to leave the album on a table and invite people who are interested to look through the pictures after the demonstration.

EVIDENCE GIVEN ON MOBILE

The portrait below was drawn at a service in the Rochester Square Temple, in May 2007. Soon after I started drawing, and the portrait of the woman below appeared on the paper, two women raised their hands, saying that it might be for them.

They both also accepted the descriptions given; the character of the person, the age of passing into spirit and the illness that the person suffered from before her passing. It can be confusing sometimes if there is more than one potential recipient who is able to accept both the portrait and the verbal information provided.

18- Edith M. W. (H.) 1920- 2006 (Drawn 26.5.2007)

I then heard the name 'Andrew' and I repeated it out loud. It was only then that one of the women smiled and said she definitely can accept it as firm evidence. At the end of the service, she came over to collect the drawing and showed me her mobile phone on which she pointed to a photograph of a young man with an elderly lady who was clearly in bed. Both were smiling.

"This is my son Andrew together with my mother," she said.

The photograph was one of the last taken in the hospital shortly before her mother's passing.

A BIRTHDAY PRESENT

I believe there are no coincidences in life. Life constantly brings new opportunities to us. It is then left to us to see and act on them. When we do, we open new doors into our lives. But if we do not, possibly because, at the time, we may be preoccupied with trying to control our lives, or too busy to see the alternatives presented to us, I believe they will be presented to us again sometime in the future. They will keep coming until we are ready to take note and possibly act on them.

At my demonstrations, there may not be sufficient time for each person in the room to receive messages from their loved ones in spirit. However, I find that some of the messages given to the others would be such that they also needed to hear. These messages would not be personal in the sense of relating to individuals in their lives but, rather, relating to their attitudes and ways of dealing with issues. In other words, there would be a common 'theme' to the messages given that all needed to hear.

It is as if all those present were brought in together because they had to hear the wisdom in the messages passed on. After the demonstration, some share their own stories with me. Others, even though they have not received any direct messages, express gratitude for being there. Often they have said that though they were not initially planning to come, at the last minute, someone called and invited them, or they met a friend on the street, and decided to join in. It is almost as if they were made to come and hear the message.

Some challenges in life, such as illness or death, may make us feel very vulnerable, exposed and alone. It is usually at these times that we realise that we cannot always control life and the emotions that these events bring up to the surface; yet, we have to face them. This is when we usually would allow even the faintest possibility of a 'miracle' to enter into our lives. A recent loss of someone close to us, or a serious illness that we or someone close to us is facing, often inspires us to question life and death.

The next story is one such little 'miracle' story — as the recipient had never previously visited a Spiritualist church. It was her and her family's first experience with Spirit communication.

19- Inez M. R. 1925- 2010 (Drawn 9.5.10)

The portrait above was made at the Wimbledon Spiritualist Church and both the drawing and the verbal information were accepted with gratitude by a young woman. She was with her husband and a young daughter. I did not know at the time that she had only just, in the previous two weeks, lost her mother. The portrait was of her mother. Her mother not only communicated and provided her portrait as an evidence of her continuing life but also made it an extra-special precious gift to her daughter, as it was her birthday.

THE FIRST CONTACT

Some of the sittings I do are for people who have never experienced spirit communication before. Sometimes, they are anxious about what to expect and also whether it is the right thing to do. Many of them might be in mourning. Some seem to be full of doubt; others come with an open-minded scepticism. I always hope that they will be able to leave with a big smile and a firm belief. It is a great pleasure to be able to give them the evidence that their loved ones did not just disappear but survived death — because life is eternal.

The most precious gift any communication gives is the inspiration to question our lives. It is the wake-up call for everything that we have taken for granted until then. It encourages us to question our values, why we do the things the way we do and behave the way we behave. Such an experience never fails to lead the way to a new understanding, which could eventually bring real meaning into our lives.

In January 2013, I was visiting Turkey for a demonstration, which was being filmed as part of a documentary by the Turkish Television and Radio Corporation entitled *At the Edge of Science*. The day before, I was asked to give a private sitting to the family of a good friend. I especially ask people not to give me any information about why I am asked to do a sitting.

In this case it turned out to be for a mother and young daughter. They had not had such an experience before and were both excited, not knowing what to expect. I include the letter I later received from the daughter below.

20- Kemal T. 1951- 2012 (Drawn 11.1.2013)

"The message we received from my recently deceased father was the most incredible and compelling experience that anyone could have.

"To contact my dear father through Esi was very special.... Similarly it was equally special to get to know Esi through my father. Although most people around me would feel uncomfortable with anything spiritual, I was quite amenable, and having met Esi, and having had the experience, I am reassured that there is no reason to waver. In my view, it is a unique experience that has to be lived/witnessed by anyone who misses their loved ones whom they've lost.

Dear Esi, I give you my boundless love and thanks for this, Ceren T."

REGRETS FROM A MOTHER-IN-LAW

This portrait drawn at Clapham Spiritualist Church in October 2009 was accepted by a friend of mine. I met her through the Heath Hands, a charitable preservation society, whose volunteers work on Hampstead Heath at the weekends. I met her husband several times but did not know anything about either of their families.

My friend had never been to a Spiritualist church until I invited her to one of my services. She did not appear to be entirely convinced with my explanations but said she would come with an open mind.

One of the drawings was of a woman whom I did not feel would be a friendly person, but rather someone with a very critical attitude to life. She was sitting with her arms crossed and not smiling. When I described what I was seeing, my friend smiled and said that she was her late mother-in-law.

21- Julka R. 1885- 1970 (Drawn 24.10.2009)

The mother in-law then smiled a sad smile, and expressed her regrets not only for being unfriendly towards her daughter in-law, but also for not appreciating the precious life she was given.

My friend told me later that her husband came from a Jewish family from Vienna who fled because of the political situation in 1934. The husband's mother had been reluctant to flee, and my friend said she disliked everything, including her. She found fault with my friend constantly and she lived with them all the time as the husband was killed in an accident.

All the messages I so far received show me that those in spirit have one experience in common. It appears that following passing, they not only review their past life on earth, but also realise that yes, they were playing 'roles' they had chosen before incarnating on earth. Importantly, they seem to recognise that they always had choices, some of which — had they exercised them differently — would have ensured they did not to have the regrets they were now expressing.

Such messages are always profound and they help to heal the pain and sadness people left behind on earth have been carrying throughout their lives.

SHE DIED IN HER DREAM!

The drawing below was sketched during a service at Hampton Hill Spiritualist Church in July 2008.

As soon as I finished drawing I could see a lovely elderly lady standing by with a smile on her face. A young woman recognised the person in the portrait immediately as her grandmother who had very recently passed into spirit. The grandmother was someone with such a sense of humour that everyone was soon smiling.

22- Irene B. 1922-2008 (Drawn 27.7.2008)

I sensed that she passed into spirit while she was asleep, and offered the information to the young lady to ascertain whether it was the case. As it was being accepted by the granddaughter I heard the older woman correcting me. "In my dream!"

It makes you wonder!

REGRETS FROM A FATHER

A young lady who had previously received portraits from me at some other demonstrations brought her new partner to the Clapham National Spiritualist Church. I'd never met him before and knew nothing about him or his family. It was his first visit to a Spiritualist Church. A first visit does not necessarily mean a person will receive a communication from a medium, let alone a portrait. Therefore, I was happy that he seemed to have received one.

He later wrote to me, also reminding me of the evidence that was communicated to him.

23- Salomon S. J. (Drawn 28.6.2014)

"Dear Esi

"I hope you are well. I got some time to write this morning at work and I would like to tell you about your last demonstration.

"You did the portrait of a man with afro hair, moustache and a tie. My father had afro hair, always had a moustache and a tie.

"You were doing a movement with your shoulder, almost trying to imitate his way of walking, keeping your head up. My father used to do that all the time, lifting his shoulders up.

"You said that you did not feel he was my father but more like an uncle. I had the same feeling because my father left my mom when I was 15 and he started a new family with another young woman and had other kids.

"You said that he had a lot of responsibilities and he says he wishes he could have taken a different role in his life but he was in difficult circumstances. The young woman left him and he ended up alone.

"You mentioned that this man had an operation around his stomach that caused him problems with his walking which was also true.

"You also mentioned that someone in the family broke their arm. He broke my mother's arm when they were still together.

"I do not have very many pictures of him and went through some old ones but they were all very small. I enclose one. Maybe you would be interested to see the resemblance.

Toju S."

10 - YOU AS THE MESSENGER

The demonstrations do not always follow the same order. Sometimes, the person in the drawing may not be recognised but the verbal information given may be accepted by a recipient. This may appear to be rather confusing to the potential recipient but there is a reason. It is because Spirit may wish to reach someone not present in the room, and someone in the room could act as a messenger. In that case, the verbal information given would be such that it will guide the 'messenger' to the owner of the drawing.

The reason they want to reach those who are not present may be two-fold. It may be because they are ill (and therefore unable to make it to the service or the demonstration), and are in need of healing at the time. The Spirit may want to let them know that it was being sent to them. Or, it may be that the person they want to communicate with is someone who does not know or believe that life is eternal but that they are at a stage of their life when it would be beneficial for them to explore these ideas. By receiving a portrait drawn by a spirit artist, they may be encouraged to think about, and start questioning life and living, in a different light.

The Spirit may also do that by guiding me to draw the portrait of someone who is still alive (as in some of the examples above). Here are a few more examples, from different churches, which clearly illustrate the reasons. Some of these do not have the drawings or photographs to accompany them as they were not returned to me but even despite that, they illustrate the point.

In some of the examples, I was amazed how the sketches were traced back to the owner as the feedback I received from them shows. It seems Spirit would arrange their message to be delivered not only to the right person but also at the right time.

THE FIRST MESSENGER

In February 2005, I was at a demonstration at SAGB given by Alan Acton. One of the three women sitting together received a message. While I do not remember the details of the message, as I was drawing I felt that the portrait belonged to them. After the demonstration, I showed it to one of the women and enquired whether she recognised the person. She did not respond immediately but wanted to take it with her.

Some time later I received a photograph of a young lady taken at her wedding and the following letter. I was not given the full names.

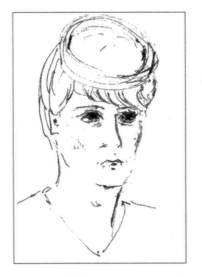 

24- Name not given 1941- ... (Drawn 20.2.2005)

"At a session on 20/02 you did this drawing for a woman called M.... and asked her if she could provide a photograph of the person it related to.

"M... is my boyfriend's ex-wife and we believe the picture has an extreme likeness to my mother.

"I have enclosed a photograph from her wedding which was 39 years ago, but as you can see her hair is very similar with

the fringe going in the same direction although the scull cap is further back on her head, but in those days she said that she always wore pillar box hats which would relate to your drawing.

"My mom and family [have] seen your sketch and were very surprised at the likeness and wondered what the connection would be with M... (my boyfriend G... is distantly related to my mum, so she had met M... a couple of times when [she] and G... were married, but nothing other than that)

"Hopefully we may get some answers from the photo. Thank you, J.M."

I remember writing back and explaining that we all may be used as messengers for someone else. I could not recall much of the message given to me as I was listening to the medium, and I was not trying to communicate directly myself; I was simply inspired to draw and that is what I did.

Her mother's drawing was the first of my portraits that the Spirit passed on through someone else acting as the messenger. I did not find out why, or even who the communicator was. Maybe their answer was in the messages they received from the medium.

I, myself, found out why a few years later, as the next story illustrates.

A WARNING FOR THE BROTHER

I believe that there is a rich variety of reasons why Spirit wants to communicate with us — not only to provide us with evidence of life after death, but also to show us how those in spirit are involved in our daily lives and are willing to help and support each one of us. The following is one of these stories which shows how they may simply want to help.

25- Lucio 1965 - 1994 (Drawn 28.6.2014)

It was at the Clapham National Spiritualist Church in June 2014 when I drew this portrait of a young man. The drawing was recognised by a lady who informed me that she knows his family and that she would pass the drawing and the message to his brother. I will let her explain, in her own words:

(A.F., 2.7.2014)

"The portrait was of a young man, tall and long limbed, who passed away in his late 20s.

"I recognised him....he has something similar to an old friend of mine, who came to me years ago in a spiritual centre in Hyde Park Corner.... it was my first message ever from spirit world.

"His name is Lucio. Tall, skinny, more beautiful than the portrait (as you said), passed when he was 29.... almost 20 years ago. The message he wanted to deliver was for someone in the family...someone who has problems with his lungs... problems with breathing. He takes the cigarette and throws it away. It means he wants to tell this person to stop smoking.

"He also wanted to say to believe in the spiritual world because it will help him to get better and heal. He has to believe because spirits have been trying to communicate before.

"Well, I passed this message to my friend, the brother of Lucio…. he confirmed everything…. there was no way I could have known this….

"Apparently he has been coughing a lot recently. He had a pain in his lungs. He has been smoking more then usual and he cannot stop. His partner has been very worried about him and she has been trying to convince him to get checked. On Saturday he was having a shower after work; he coughed and some blood came out of his mouth…. he thought it was coming from his gums… but when he coughed again …. more blood. The message was definitely for him. He really appreciated this message and he thanked me, and he thanked you. He asked me to give you a big hug from him.

"Regarding spirituality… he told me he recently had a dream about his father in spirit and he was smiling and happy… and when he woke up he was very relieved and at peace with himself. He thinks that was a message too.

"I send you the photo of Lucio…. when he was healthy…. and after two years of chemo for Leukaemia which killed him.

"This is an amazing story Esi. You are amazing."

Spirit uses such opportunities to the fullest. At the beginning of my demonstrations, I like to point out that Spirit is always around us and would like us to know that. Unless we are open to the idea that life is continuous and the communication is possible, we would ignore any feelings, sounds, or visions we may be receiving and regard them as 'coincidence'. It must really be rather frustrating for the Spirit to be an invisible person!

I also know that the way of Spirit is to respect the decisions we make in this material world; that is why we are in this life — to make choices. Some will be the right ones while others will not. It is through our daily experiences and the choices we make that we learn and spiritually grow. There are times when we all feel confused, lonely and in need of some direction. I know that if we ask, we will always receive help even if not in ways we may like to hear! The reason is that Spirit will not tell us what we want to know, but what we need to know.

As someone who has gifts for communication with Spirit as well as the capacity to be guided by Spirit to provide portraits of those in spirit or even alive, I have come to know that each demonstration is a different experience for me too — each one also brings a lesson for me. After every church service or demonstration, I always ask myself what it was that I could learn this time!

I remember, when I first started working with Spirit, I questioned why I did not start this work much earlier in my life! Now, looking back and recalling the many spirit communications and the portraits given, I can see clearly why I had to wait till later in my life. I first had to experience life and wait for my own development through life. I do appreciate that our experiences are what shape us into the people we are. Each one of us has a role to play in our lives.

My experiences now allow me to have empathy with a larger number of people both on earth and in spirit, which in turn facilitates my ability to provide communication between them.

11 - MUSIC AND THE COMPOSERS

Music, especially classical music, was a big part of my life as a child. My father once told me that it had been his childhood dream to become a conductor. However, while he was still at university, he lost his father and two of his siblings, and as he was the oldest son, he had to take care of his family — his sister, brother and his mother. So, he became a lecturer in Mathematics and Astronomy, and turned away from pursuing a career in music.

He was also an artist, writer, poet, and musician (he played the violin). While going through some papers I found two of his score books in his library. On the corner of the first page of one of them was a note stating that it was purchased with the very first money he had earned as an assistant lecturer at the university. On the first pages my father had hand-copied music by Nikolai Rimsky-Korsakov, but towards the end I came across a page with two small pieces written for me. One was called 'Lullaby to Esi' and the other 'Esi's dance'. Even though he had written these a few years before I was born, he later placed a photograph of me, taken when I was about eight months old, holding his violin.

26- Esi's Dance

I have fond memories of listening to classical music with my parents when I was very young. My father would play from his large collection of classical music records while my young brother and I sat on the floor. He would tell us stories about swans and horses, making the music come alive in our little minds as we listened. My mother used to tell me how she liked watching our smiles and excitement, though there were also times when she found it difficult to stay with us when the stories would be sad and she'd see the tears roll down our cheeks.

Later, I was given lessons by a music-teacher friend of my father. My mother made sure that I practised daily but I still remember the teacher gently hitting on my fingers with his baton (which I found rather offensive!) if I had not practised enough or made mistakes. I think my piano lessons lasted only about a year or two but, later, in our teenage years, both my brother and I started learning the classical guitar. My brother, however, preferred pop music and was to start his own band. I later had a try at playing the drums in the hope that, maybe, I would be invited to join! Obviously playing an instrument was not my gift as the invitation was not made! Soon, though, I was into fashion and dancing, and I helped the band members with movements to do on stage. I also went to a modelling school and started modelling for fashion shows on the catwalk while still at the university.

I was in my twenties when I became aware that I could not identify the names of the composers of pieces I heard playing! While I could follow the music closely, I was unable to give the names! It was only then I realised that it was because I always had someone playing the music at home; first my father playing classical music, then in our teenage years my brother, playing mostly the psychedelic music of 1960s!

National folk music was not listened to at home, and I was therefore not much acquainted with it. Although I liked it, I regarded it as only part of the cultural heritage.

Late one night in the autumn of 2002 when I was visiting my mother in Istanbul, I heard an old folk song. On each of the following nights I heard it again. It would always happen late at night: I would go to bed, and just before falling asleep, I would hear this particular folk song being softly sung by a man. My mother lived on a first floor flat. Each time I heard it, I got up out of bed and looked out of the window, trying to determine where the sound could be coming from. I checked whether anyone had parked their car outside our window, and was listening to their radio, but I could not see anybody outside. Neither could I clearly hear the words of the song, though it sounded like a song from the eastern region of Turkey.

At the end of my visit, I returned to London. I had sold my flat and was staying with friends in Hampstead. My bedroom was in the back of the house and it was a very quiet room. On the first night back, once again, just before falling asleep, I began to hear the same song! This happened a few more days and I could not make any sense of why I was hearing it.

Over the next six months, I completely refurbished the flat I had bought. During the refurbishments, I had several tradesmen involved in the site works. I spent most of the days in the flat, supervising their work. One morning, I arrived at the flat and found one of the men singing the same song!

He was a friendly Turkish man with Kurdish origins. He was from a village close to a city named Kars in the eastern region of Turkey where I was born. I have no recollection of the place as my parents had been assigned to teach there for a short time when they were new graduates. It had been the Government's education policy to appoint young graduate teachers on a short-term basis to the eastern parts of Turkey in order to increase the level of literacy in the country.

This young builder used to tell me about his mother who apparently was a good horse rider and also very good with guns! He told me that he had travelled to the UK and lied in order to enter the country. He said he came to the UK as a refugee, claiming that as a Kurdish man, would be put into jail if he went back to Turkey. This, he confessed to me, was not true!

In fact, he had always been very honest with me, once informing me that by mistake he had damaged some pipes that would later be hidden from sight behind some wall cladding. Had he not told me of this there would have been water damage in the future and it would have been a very costly exercise to locate and repair the problem.

I always wondered if hearing the singing first in Istanbul, and then later in London, was a premonition of some sort. Could it be that I tuned into the future, or the past, or both? The reason I consider that as a possibility is because there is even a stranger story that followed.

It was during my stay with the same friends. One morning, my friend Cem, who is a conductor, told me that he had been invited for lunch by another conductor friend at his place. As he was leaving, he said he would stop by the post office on his way. After a while, the phone rang. It was his friend inquiring when Cem left home, and complaining that as Cem was late, his food would be ruined. I calmed him down and assured him that Cem should be there very soon. However, to ensure that all was well with him, I decided to call Cem on his mobile. The phone did not ring but it was answered immediately. I heard Cem and his friend talking as if he had just arrived, and I could also hear some classical music playing in the background. I called his name few times but received no response. However, having heard him arrive safely at his friend's house, I was satisfied and put the phone down.

Later, when Cem came back, I asked him why he hadn't answered when I called his mobile phone. He seemed confused and said he never received any calls from me or anybody else. In fact, he added, his phone never even rang. He checked his mobile and there were no 'missed' or 'received' calls that morning. I then questioned if there was any music playing at his friend's place and he replied that no, there wasn't. It seems I tuned in to hear his safe arrival!!

In 2004, I had just started drawing portraits with Spirit but never expected to be inspired to do one outside a demonstration or church service, let alone during a classical concert. But that is what happened, and it came as a total surprise. What's more, the first time I was inspired in this way, it turned out to be one of the composers whose music was being played at the concert.

WOLFGANG AMADEUS MOZART

27- Wolfgang Amadeus Mozart 1756- 1791 (Drawn 26.4.2004)
Statue by Austrian Viktor Tilgner, Vienna, Austria, 1896
Credit: Dreamstime LLC

I was attending a concert at the Barbican Centre in April 2004. The conductor was my friend, Cem Mansur. Soon after the concert started I began drawing.

I could sense that this man had powdered hair. After the concert, meeting Cem backstage, I asked him "which composer would have had powdered hair?" He looked down at the drawing I'd made and said it could only be Mozart, whose music they were playing. As soon as I arrived back home, I went online to look at the composers' images and here it was. I had been guided to draw the portrait of Mozart! Was he there listening with us?

JEAN SIBELIUS AND ROALD DAHL

The second time I was inspired to do a portrait at a concert hall was in September 2004. In a production at the Barbican, Roald Dahl's last story, *The Minpins*, was narrated over a score taken from Jean

Sibelius, arranged and conducted by Peter Ash. I believe the portrait I did was of Roald Dahl himself. I quite like the idea that he joined us at the concert!

28- Roald Dahl 1916- 1990 (Drawn 28.9.2004)

GEORG FRIEDRICH HANDEL

On another occasion I went to a festival at St. John's, Smith Square, London in October 2005. The festival was held at this 300-year-old building, which is a fine example of English Baroque architecture. It was restored both as a church and concert hall in the late 1960s with exceptional acoustics.

During the performance, I was inspired again: this time, to draw two portraits, one of a woman with long hair gathered in the back, and a portrait of a gentleman wearing a wig.

29- Georg Friedrich Händel 1685- 1759 (Drawn 3.1.2006)
Monument by Hermann Heidel, Halle (Saale), Germany. 1859
Credit: Dreamstime LLC

A friend, Chris Tudor, was the choreographer for one of the ballet pieces — Händel's *Cantate Amorosa.*

I showed him both of the drawings after the performance. Chris was amazed. He said the woman had a good resemblance to one of his tutors when he was studying ballet and who had passed into spirit some time ago. And, he said, the gentleman reminded him of Händel.

Back at home, I went online and I found photograph of the monument shown in figure 29. Here he was, with a good likeness to the portrait I had done earlier. I thought it was the best compliment they could give to my friend; the teacher and the composer, both attending his performance!

ANTONIO VIVALDI

In December 2007, I was again visiting my mother when I was invited to a concert at the Caddebostan Concert Hall in Istanbul. Cem Mansur

101

was the conductor and the guest soloist, playing violin, was Alexander Markov. Alex, as he is known among his friends, is an extremely gifted and well-respected musician, and I had met him on previous occasions.

Alex was playing the Four Seasons by Vivaldi when I knew I had to do a sketch.

30- Antonio Vivaldi 1678 - 1741 (Drawn 26.12.2007)
Engraving by Francois Morellon la Cave, 1725
Credit: Lebrecht Music + Arts.

My father often used to play this piece and it usually brings tears to my eyes when I listen to it. So I was happy to have my attention drawn to doing a portrait. At the time, Alex was standing in front, in the middle of the stage, playing beautifully. However, as I sketched the portrait, I also felt I was being 'taken out' of the concert hall and into another space.

I could not see anything but felt the vastness of this space as it started filling with the music. I am not sure how long it lasted, possibly seconds, but I was enthralled. It was an overwhelming surprise. I still find it impossible to describe the music played; the quality of sound, the depth and the clarity. But, I somehow knew that I was listening to Vivaldi playing his piece!

Equally disappointing was coming back into the concert hall.

Suddenly, I was back and the music I was hearing was so flat! Later, when I went backstage to meet my friend and Alex, and congratulate the orchestra after the concert, I told him how lucky he is to be a musician, as he will have the most incredible surprise when he does the passing into his next part of his life!

NICCOLO PAGANINI

In April 2008, at yet another concert I was again inspired to do the portrait below. The concert was at the intimate Purcell Room at the Queen Elizabeth Hall, Southbank, London, and included two visiting musicians from Turkey: Ahmet Kaneci (guitar), and Ekrem Oztan (clarinet).

During the Sonata Concertata by Paganini, as I started drawing a gentleman I could also see him. He was very slim with very long limbs. He had long hair and was dressed all in black. He was wearing a long black coat and was playing the violin.

The first violin player of his time at the
National Theatre in Nurnberg, 1829
31- Niccolo Paganini 1782 - 1840 (Drawn 7.4.2008)
Credit: Lebrecht Music + Arts

This time, I was only receiving visual images but not the audio as I could not hear the music he was playing. However, it was so real. I knew I was watching Paganini playing his violin.

Back at home I searched again on the Internet. Here it was, I found several images of him wearing black exactly as I'd seen him!

JOHANN SEBASTIAN BACH

The Parish Church of St John-at-Hampstead Church Row, London is a famous and popular venue for classical concerts. It is recorded that there has been a church on this site for a thousand years. The present church is part of the Anglican Community, consecrated around 1747, and has a War Memorial and a famous graveyard. They hold regular church services as well as literary events and concerts, both at lunch time and in the evening.

In May 2008 I went to a concert there given by the world-famous pianist Stephen Kovacevich. He lives in Hampstead and I had met him previously through my conductor friend.

This time, I was inspired to do a portrait only, while Kovacevich was playing Bach. I also felt that the person I was drawing was wearing a wig. My usual online search did not disappoint! The image below shows a strong resemblance to the portrait.

32- Johann Sebastian Bach 1685- 1750 (Drawn 14.5.2008)
Monument in front of the Thomas Church
(Thomaskirche), Leipzig, Germany
Credit: Dreamstime LLC.

LUDWIG VAN BEETHOVEN

Beethoven's music was often played in our house when I was growing up. Later, after I started at the university, I recall a conversation on classical music with two friends. One of them studied classical guitar, and asked me who my favourite composer was. I remember saying Beethoven, as I felt his music was very close to my heart; it calmed me down. Both of my friends objected, saying it is not the kind of music to calm anyone down! At the time, I could not respond to them to justify why and how; all I knew was that it was how it made me feel.

On this occasion, I was at home in London, listening to the Classic FM radio station. I cannot recall the piece but remember receiving mental images, and feeling as if I was in a room where there was a big and rather high, unmade bed with white sheets and large pillows. I was seeing this very emotional young man in the room. It was as if he spent a lot of time in this room and was writing music. He was Beethoven.

Having had this emotional connection with Beethoven, and feeling the emotional turmoil he was in very strongly, I suddenly knew why I could not explain to my friends my reasons why his music had a calming effect on me.

Having seen and felt his emotions in that room as I listened to his music, I realised that his music 'spoke' to me in such a way that it made me feel I was not alone, and that was at an age when I was not even aware I felt lonely! Talking to my friends at the time, all I knew was that I felt a certain rapport with, and affinity for, his music.

33- Ludwig Van Beethoven 1770- 1827 (Drawn 14.3.2009)
Statue by Caspar Clemons Von Zumbush, Vienna, Austria. 1880
Credit: Dreamstime LLC.

My journey into discovering events that played a huge part in who I was to become as a person — formulating the questions to ask, and finally finding the answers to the questions — took a long time. It had been a lengthy and, at times, painful journey. That journey now enables me to be in empathy with, and to relate to, more people both in this world and the next. But I found it amazing that Spirit was also helping me with answers to my long-standing questions. In this case, they gave me the answer through my communication with Beethoven!

PART 3

HEALING

Looking back, I see how incredibly lucky I have been, having spent the first half of my life with no serious illnesses or deaths either in my family or even in the wider circle of relatives and friends.

Following my master's degree, I moved to London in 1978, hoping to gain some work experience. It was not long before I was offered a position with the RHWL Partnership as an Urban Designer.

After two years, I was offered another job with an International Design office, IDEA International Ltd (IDEA), owned by a Saudi architect. There was, at the time, a major development and construction phase underway in Saudi Arabia, and the office was commissioned to design 22 new towns for the Internal Security Forces Housing Development.

A London office was set up in addition to the existing regional offices in the USA, Greece, France and Saudi Arabia. In London, I was the first person to be employed after the Director, and was the last one to leave when they closed it six years later. I was initially employed as the urban designer for the new town projects but later I designed most of the large-scale competitions. This marked the start of the international phase of my professional life.

About a year into my employment, I found out I had thyroid cancer. The diagnostic biopsy was followed by an operation after which I lost my voice for about a month. It was a difficult time, but it helped me to give up smoking! By the end of the month, I no longer felt any cravings for nicotine — as if it had been erased from my mind.

No previous experience with the medical world must have made me feel especially brave because I did not inform my family, except my brother. I did not wish to worry my parents! At the time, the cancer was considered almost a 'death sentence' as not much was openly written about, or discussed, in public. My brother had also recently qualified as an architect. He was married and living in Munich, Germany, while working on his PhD. We had always been very close and supportive of each other.

My parents did not know about my illness until a month later when I visited them to recuperate in their summer place. The scar on my neck was still covered with a gauze pad because it had not yet healed. They were shocked when I explained the situation to them although they did try not to make a big issue of it. My grandmother visited us soon after. When she saw the bandage, she asked about it. I had assumed that my parents had already told her, so I replied simply, almost off-handedly, "You know, the cancer operation." She looked at me with widened eyes, and then said, "Of course not, an insect must have bitten you!"

Until my illness, I did not have much time for, or interest in, the alternative approaches to the maintenance of good health or the possible cure of illnesses. I was unaware of any of the critical views that claimed that the radical treatments of physical illnesses had become merely the treatment of symptoms.

Shortly after my operation, I started having acupuncture treatments and I continue to this day. I was impressed with how quickly I began to experience the changes. I remember saying to my wonderful acupuncturist, Nora Franglen, that I felt as if someone with a bucket of oil and a large brush was oiling all my joints! I simply felt lighter and more energetic. I also remember her response, which was that it is because I was now more 'balanced.'

I became a great admirer of traditional Chinese medicine. Wanting to learn more about it, I started going to Nora's lectures at the Mary Ward Centre in Bloomsbury. Her lectures were not about how to become an acupuncturist but what acupuncture was all about. Her master was J. R. Worsley, who would visit her surgery twice a year to see some of her patients. They practised Five Element Acupuncture.

Both Nora and Worsley contributed a lot to my understanding of the 'concept of health in body, mind and spirit'. I was particularly impressed by the statement in Worsley's book, *Is Acupuncture for You?* (1973 USA, 1985 UK):

"Only Nature can cure disease. Practitioners only assist Nature, acting as instruments of Nature by putting the patient back on the path to health ... Acupuncture can do so much to help fight and prevent disease but maintaining health is not solely the responsibility of the doctor or practitioners; for the most part it is our own."

The more I learned about the philosophy on which Chinese medicine is based, the more impressed I was. As my contribution to acupuncture, I translated Worsley's book into Turkish as *Saglikli Bir Yasam Icin Akupunktur* (2001).

At the time, digital communication systems as we know them now did not exist. The information on ideas or research could be distributed to and learned by the wider community only through printed media such as books and magazines. The pioneering studies in Science, Medicine and Parapsychology might have been conducted at major universities in the USA in 1960s; however it was not until the late 1980s that books introducing new ideas were widely published. Public interest in 'self help' started soon after.

My early interests were in Psychology. I read the book the *Games People Play* (1964) in the late 1960s and found it fascinating. It was by Dr

Eric Berne (1910-1970) who had been a prominent psychiatrist and was the creator of Transactional Analysis. He argued that everyone's life follows a predetermined script which they compose themselves during early childhood. In another of his books, *What Do You Say After You Say Hello?* he demonstrates his theory with illustrations.

Thomas A Harris, in his book *I'm OK, You're OK* (1967) sought to simplify Berne's theories, and was intended as a practical guide for people to understand how their 'life position' affects their relationships and communications with others. It was one of the earliest self-help books that I read.

However, it was not until the late 1980s, long after my operation, that I read *Heal Your Body* and *You Can Heal Your Life* (1984) by Louise Hay who self-published them and later founded Hay House Publishers. They were the next popular self help books that I came across.

Life became extremely busy soon after my operation. I was involved in large-scale projects in Saudi Arabia, and started travelling between London and the office in Athens, Greece. The London office had grown rapidly and the number of staff was soon increased to 170. I was still the only female designer!

In 1981, one of the iconic architectural buildings, the King Abdul Aziz International Hajj Terminal by the prestigious firm Skidmore, Owings and Merrill (SOM) in Jeddah was completed. Soon after, a member of the Royal Family, inspired by the fabric-roofed structure of the terminal building, commissioned IDEA International to design his new house, and requested that a fabric-roofed guesthouse be included in its design.

Prior to this project, I had been the designer and the team leader for a design competition for the Equine Centre in Riyadh, Saudi Arabia. The design included extensive fabric structures shading approximately 500,000 square metres of floor area, reinterpreting the traditional Bedouin tents. I include a section view of the project below to give a sense of large scale of the development. On the left is the registry office with a viewing platform. A polo field links it to the Equine Village where all the social facilities are located: a show arena, the auction arena, the museum, the mosque, administrative facilities and shops. A number of paddocks were located throughout the site.

34- Section through the Equine Centre

Having worked with tent structure specialists, Future Tents Ltd, in New York, I was asked to come up with a concept design for a guesthouse to be integrated to the site of the main residence, which was being designed in the Athens office.

I travelled to the Athens office and, once the concept design of both schemes was completed, I flew to Singapore with the designer of the main residence to meet the client who not only accepted my proposal for the guest house but also, because he was so taken with the design, started adding more and more spaces from the main house into the guest house. Eventually, my project became the main house!

I began working on the project in 1983, which was designed as an earth-sheltered building with extensive landscaping over the roof slab, hiding the structure from view. Entry into the house was through the short walls cut into the landscaping. Two tent structures covered the main reception and the master bedroom. It was the first time in the world that tensile structures were being used in a residential building. It has been one of my favourite projects and was to keep me busy until 1988.

The construction of the Red Sea Residence was completed in 1986 and soon after, the IDEA International closed down its London office. The client then asked me to stay with the project, and supervise the interior finishes of the building, which was designed by the legendary Interior Designer Bill Willis (1937 - 2009) who lived in Marrakesh. His proposals were to be carried out by Moroccan artisans who were not used to reading technical drawings!

Bill had worked successfully with them on smaller scale buildings but the scale and complexity of the Red Sea project was such that it was

111

necessary for me to assist and coordinate. Consequently, I commuted from London to Jeddah every month for 18 months until the site works had been completed.

35- The entrance court, side elevation, and aerial view from the sea

Towards the end of 1980s the recession in the UK was beginning to take hold. Even though I was still busy supervising the interior finishes, most of my architect friends had been made redundant in London and I knew that my work would soon draw to an end and that jobs in the UK were becoming increasingly difficult to find. Fortunately for me, once back in London, my earnings from the Red Sea residence and my savings kept me going for a while, but soon I found myself with nothing to do to fill my time. So much so that I started to feel depressed.

At that stage, I was not aware that through our lives, we all might have events such as major health issues, death, loss of jobs, or other unexpected or unplanned changes that shake us out of our comfort zone. These force us to reconsider the priorities, beliefs and values by which we live our lives.

During the time I was working on the interiors, I'd been renting a shared studio in the Covent Garden area of London. When the project was near completion, I started working from home. My flat, a Victorian conversion, had very high ceilings. As my studio, I used the living room, which had a large window facing the garden. The other window in the room was a rather narrow, tall one along the sidewall, and facing the staircase of the neighbouring School. I lived in that flat for seven years, and had kept the roller blind drawn over that window to maintain some privacy.

I remember clearly waking up one morning and walking into my studio feeling extremely frustrated with nothing to do. I kept asking myself, again and again "who am I if not an architect?" — but I could not answer that question. It seemed that I was only an architect and an urban designer; that is what filled my days, my life. That was all I could do with my life! Yes, I was good at it, but with the job market drying up, what would I do now?

I felt frustrated, I felt depressed, I felt confused, but, looking back, I was not consciously aware of not having panic attacks anymore. I can only see now that all the hard work on my past emotional life through the years of psychotherapy, did release me from the vicious circle of holding on to the life scenarios I designed as a child. I was no longer held prisoner by them.

As I was walking up and down the flat, trying to find an answer, my eyes were drawn to the top of the narrow window in my living room, and suddenly I thought of drawing the blind to let the light in!

The idea of such a simple act's making so significant a change caused me to smile. It brought more light into the room both physically and figuratively — lifting my mood and making me realise that one needs to be creative in life as a whole, not only in what we are trained to do. And somehow, it gave me hope to carry on!

12- MY EMOTIONAL JOURNEY

Having been born into a highly educated and artistic family, I was fortunate, throughout my childhood and teenage years, to have enjoyed a relatively privileged life. We were raised to value family, culture, and education more than money and material possessions. Most of my memories from my childhood are of happy times: playing outside in the gardens and the fields, climbing trees and running wild.

Looking back, I can see that I was growing up to be an independent child even if this was not due to any conscious effort on my parents' part. On the contrary, I now know with the benefit of hindsight that this happened as a reaction to them; my parents were always too busy to 'hear' the emotional needs of a little girl. My mother herself was sent to boarding school from the age of six. Not being brought up by her mother, she did not learn how to be a mother herself by example. She had an 'ideal mother' in her mind who would care and provide the best for her children but 'hearing them' was not included in that role. In retrospect, I characterise my relationship with my mother as a constrained one.

My father used to tell us that he had an extremely authoritarian father when he was growing up. It seems that, early on at least, he closely followed in his father's footsteps both when he first started his own family and equally in his working life as a lecturer and administrator. However, he relaxed much more as we grew up; besides, he loved children and could be extremely patient with them. As he grew older, his best friends were children. He wrote over 400 children's stories, radio plays, musicals, and poems — mostly during the last 20 years of his life.

My parents, having met at the university, were very close to each other, more so than they were to their children. My independence grew out of the distance I obviously felt with regard to my parents while growing up and I must have decided that 'if they do not need me, I do not need them either'! My life is full of stories to show that. I was testing my independence in an ever-expanding range of environments as I grew up.

As children, we went through long periods of separation from our parents. First, my father was away for about a year to do his military service when I was four years old. Later, they then spent a long time, together or individually, in the USA and the UK, doing research and training to further their professions in education. I started primary school while living with my grandmother and aunt in Istanbul because they were both away.

Later, when I was thirteen years old, my mother again went to London for research and training, though at this time I was asked whether she should take me or my brother with her. I chose to stay with my father. As I remember, I expected that I would take my mother's place whenever my father was invited to an opening of an exhibition or reception, which was often, and I imagined it was going to be a very glamorous life that I would live while standing in for her. To my disappointment, this did not turn out to be the case even though I did accompany him on few occasions. My grandmother took over the running of our home.

When I was sixteen, it was arranged for me to spend my summer holiday with my father's younger brother — an architect who, with his family, was living and working in Munich, Germany. They had a daughter few years my junior. It was my first taste of overseas travel and I enjoyed it.

My next international trip was in 1968, hitch-hiking in Europe and the UK. I had begun my studies at the Middle East Technical University, Administrative Sciences Department, where the curriculum was in English. I told my parents that I wanted to go to a youth camp in England with a girlfriend during my summer holiday in order to improve my English. Their response was that they could give me only so much money and if it would cover my expenses, I could go. But it did not! It was sufficient to buy a train ticket from Istanbul to Munich. I did not tell my parents but arranged with my brother's girlfriend who was brought up and living in Munich that we could stay with her once we arrived. We thought that it should be easy enough to hitchhike from Munich to England.

So we took the train. When we arrived in Munich, we left our suitcases with my brother's girlfriend, bought backpacks, and set off hitchhiking to England. We crossed the Channel by boat and were extremely seasick. At the entry into the country, we were given a month's visa to stay and we ended up working in the strawberry fields near Norwich.

It was a completely alien experience for us to stay in the barracks of the student camp site and to work as strawberry pickers. We enjoyed it immensely but, coming from a Mediterranean country, thought it freezing cold at night even though it was August. We each had six blankets given to us to keep warm but still could not sleep because it felt so cold. A few days later, we searched and found a little bungalow on the river with a small jetty and rented it for the remainder of our stay.

The evenings were mostly occupied by pub visits, also a new experience for us. Soon we heard that there was a fashion show planned at the student campsite. Having recently completed a modelling course in Ankara, I inquired and was invited to join them as one of the models on the catwalk. This opportunity helped me to earn some additional money. I could have made use of the photos taken that night for potential fashion modelling contracts some years later when I was looking for a job in Sydney, Australia, but unfortunately most were stolen from a friend's car after I returned home.

Our stay in the UK soon came to an end when both our visas and money ran out. An English friend suggested that we go to Paris for about a week and stay with some French friends of mine. He would then lend us some money so we could return to the UK and get another month's visa. It did not work as planned and our return to Istanbul via Paris was adventurous and at times dangerous, but we managed to hitchhike back to Istanbul. At the time, hitchhiking by young girls from Turkey was not heard of at home. Looking back, I now agree that it was not the wisest way of travelling especially when telecommunications between the countries via switchboards were so difficult. But my next overseas trip was even more daring.

Studying Administrative Sciences had never been my or my family's choice. Both my aunt and uncle had studied at the Academy of Fine Arts in Istanbul and my aunt, while I was living with them as a child, would sometimes take me to their studios and the Academy's canteen. I somehow always assumed that I would also one day attend the same institution, but when I was older and the time came for me to decide which university I would go to, we were living in Ankara. My parents were reluctant to send me to Istanbul to live alone and study.

At the time, we had to take exams to enter the university. My points qualified me to attend the prestigious Middle East Technical University (METU) in Ankara but only the Department of City Planning or Administrative Sciences rather than the Department of Architecture. There was no department of art, and architecture was not my first choice. My preference was to study art and sculpture at the Academy of Fine Arts in Istanbul. Disappointed that my parents did not allow me to study in Istanbul, I chose the department of Administrative Sciences. I was soon bored and disillusioned. I found that I was no good at writing extensive articles about theories that I thought could have been explained in few simple sentences.

However, I met my future husband who was also in my year and we started dating. In my second year at METU, he and I started thinking about emigrating to Australia. His brother's sister-in-law and her husband had applied to move to Australia after finishing their studies and their applications were accepted, and we liked the idea. The fact that the travelling expenses to Australia would be met by the Australian government made it even more attractive. However, I did not think I could even discuss it with my parents as they had refused to allow me to study in the USA only a few years earlier.

I had some American friends whose parents were employed at the American Embassy near our house in Ankara. A few years earlier, my close friend Laura, who was my age, and her family were moving back to the USA. Her parents offered that I could stay with them should my parents allow me to study in the USA — an idea that was not completely foreign to me, given that both my parents had travelled and studied in the USA and the UK while I was growing up. I was happy to follow in their footsteps but my parents would not allow it.

For this reason, I was sure that studying in Australia, especially as an immigrant, was not going to meet with my parents' approval. Nevertheless, that did not stop me from going ahead and giving my application to the Australian Consulate; it simply meant that I shared my plans only with my brother, to whom I was very close.

To my parents I said only that I did not want to stay at the Department for Administrative Sciences, and would be taking exams again the following year with the object of gaining entry into the Department of Architecture. In order to convince them, I left the university and started working at an architect's office as a junior draftsperson. Learning general drafting work was to become handy a few years later when I indeed studied Architecture, but that is not something I planned at the time.

My boyfriend, on the other hand, had obtained a year off from the university and left for Holland to stay with his brother and his family in order to lodge his application to Australia from there. For him, it was not possible to apply from Turkey because he was obliged to do his military service if he stopped studying.

My application to Australia was processed earlier than my boyfriend's, and soon I was given a date to travel to Sydney: 2 February 1969. I told my parents that I was going to stay at a friend's place overnight; instead I took the plane to Sydney. My brother and a few friends took me to the airport. I had only my nightie, one change of clothes, my toothbrush and $20.00 with me!

My boyfriend arrived six months later. I had never been employed before until then and I tried my hand at different jobs until my boyfriend arrived. For the first few months, I worked just outside Sydney as an interpreter for other immigrants from Turkey. I then shared a flat with a girl friend in Sydney and worked at a hotel for a short while, then at a Malaysian restaurant for a few weeks and after that at the Kodak colour laboratories for some time.

I also started attending part-time classes at a commercial art school. I was not giving up on the idea of studying for a university degree so when my boyfriend arrived, we began our search for entry into the universities. Our stay in Sydney was cut short after about ten months when we found out that it would take us seven years to get a university degree, working part time, instead of the four years of full-time study in Turkey. We left Sydney with the decision that we would come back as soon as we had our degrees.

Both of our parents were extremely forgiving and generous, and paid our return fares. We took an Italian boat back, which took 33 days to sail across the oceans to Europe. On our return home, having 'run away' with my boyfriend, we both felt obliged to get engaged to save face for our families! Once we completed our university degrees, we married and moved to Istanbul; our marriage, however, did not survive longer than two years.

Following my divorce, I applied to Oxford to do a masters degree in urban design. I was accepted and it was a decision to change my life forever.

It was all very exciting to be studying urban design, which had been recognised only recently and was in its third year as a new discipline. The focus is on man-made environments at a scale between Architecture and Town Planning. It was created for the development of those urban spaces that previously had been dealt with by other two disciplines.

Urban design embraces wide aspects of our daily lives. I was most interested in how places are perceived by people, what are the 'images of places' they carry around in their minds, and why; how those images affect the use of these spaces; and how people interact visually and cognitively with places. This led me to expand my interest in environmental psychology and psychology of human behaviour.

Following the master's degree, I started a PhD degree on the cultural aspects of 'places', which led me to anthropology. However, I never finished it as my life suddenly became far too busy with design work.

While studying at Oxford, I shared a Victorian house in Jericho with six other post-graduate students, all doing the same degree. Four of us were from overseas. I had always been an independent child and teenager, and for this reason I did not expect my new life away from my familiar environment to cause any emotional or material hardships for me. After all, my parents were only a telephone call away and they were supporting me in every way.

The house belonged to the course director. It was the tradition of the house that one of us would go shopping, cook, serve food and wash dishes one day a week. The whole of the garden level floor was used as the kitchen and dining area. The person working in the kitchen would usually invite a guest or two as well. That meant that we enjoyed food from different parts of the world and had dinner parties six nights a week. Saturdays were free, so we could go out, or be invited somewhere else. It would usually mean being taken out by someone's visiting parents as a treat.

But I was also lonely at times. The course was largely based on the history of British architecture and planning whereas my architectural education was based on the European history of architecture and American planning. I was not familiar with all the names given as cross-references. There were times that I could not follow the arguments put forward on different concepts. I remember thinking "Surely what I am hearing cannot be such nonsense as we are all post-graduate students, successfully accepted to this course, and we should all be above a certain level of understanding! It must be me who misunderstands, possibly because of my English". So I kept quiet for the whole year. It was not until my second year when I realised that it was not my English. There were some students with ideas or concepts that did not make much sense to me!

I made lots of new friends but was also missing my friends in Turkey. Oxford is a wonderful place to study, and it became my home for a few years, but it was not a place in which I would settle down. As wonderful as it was, it was a transient place for me as it was for most of the other students. Once you completed your studies and left, the next time you visited it, the physical environment and the activities all looked the same but faces would have changed. It is a very melancholic place in that sense.

Some time into the first year, I came to the realisation that I was viewing my new environment through the eyes of my friends in Turkey. It was as if I, as a separate person, did not exist! Each time I met someone or bought anything new, I found myself questioning whether my friends in Istanbul would like the person or my purchase, and even approve!

I had many new friends but we were not close enough to discuss my feelings with them. Oxford is a cosmopolitan city with a large foreign population, and of course that helped. But being away from the environment and culture I grew up in, and not yet belonging to a new place, was becoming rather unsettling for me.

Being on my own and realising that I did not really know who I was forced me to start questioning my life. I found myself facing some discomforting feelings that were being brought to the surface. I even started questioning my parents. I recall going to my parents' summer place for the holidays, sitting on the terrace by the sea and thinking, "Who are these people that I call mother and father? Who am I?"

Back in Oxford, the emotional confusion became overpowering and I started having panic attacks. I was referred to a psychotherapist. Seven long years of on-and-off psychotherapy followed, which helped me to discover and own the emotional journey of my childhood. I also came to the understanding that children do not necessarily need to have physically or verbally abusive adults around them to be hurt!

I was seeing a very experienced elderly psychotherapist, Mrs Cousins, for analytical psychotherapy. For the first few months, it was also especially stressful for me to share my feelings with a total stranger but at least someone was listening to me. It was the start of the discovery of the emotionally turbulent times of a little girl whose memories were long buried in the past. As the major events that took place in my childhood started revealing themselves, I understood increasingly more about myself as a grown up.

One of these discoveries helped me not only in my emotional journey but in the roles I now play as healer and hypnotherapist. It showed me how some events play a major role in shaping who we are to become as a person, and how they influence the development of our own life scenarios. It also illustrates how the environment we are brought up in contributes to the future challenges we face along our life journeys.

I met with my therapist twice a week. She would always be present at our appointed time, listening to me, prompting me from time to time. After a while, I thought I had told her everything and felt we had run out things to discuss. She allowed very long pauses, just sitting there. Eventually, I told her that I did not know what else to talk about! She then asked me to tell her about my dreams.

For the next few sessions I did, but soon I run out of dreams I could easily remember as well! Until, that is, I recalled a dream I indeed had had very recently. I then slowly became aware that I'd had that dream many times before — it was a recurring dream. I found it strange that while I knew that dream so well, it seemed that it was completely out of my consciousness during the day. It took ages before I became aware of this and brought it back to my conscious mind!

At the time, I was dating someone called Pete from one of the colleges, who rowed for the Oxford team. He was so very different from my ex-husband. He was a well-built sportsman but for some reason, it was his smile that first caught my eye; he had a very big lovely smile. Soon we were becoming rather fond of each other and all was going so well. I was happy having a really fun time with him. He called me 'sunshine'.

I soon realised that since we'd started going out together, I would lie in bed and pray hard not to have that dream! The dream itself was a short one. In it, I would see the person I was dating. He would come over and kiss me on my cheek. That was it! But I somehow knew that if and when I had that dream, we would break up!

It took some effort on my therapist's part to bring the rest of the story into the light. It became evident that the dream related to my childhood. It must have been when I was three or four years old that my father went away to another city for his obligatory military service. As far as I know, it was the first time he'd been away from the family for an extended time. My mother noted in her diary that I became physically ill, missing my father. That was followed in a year or two by his overseas study trips to the USA and became part a routine separation for the next five or so years.

It seems that in the last days before his departure, my father would make sure that the time spent with me was extra special. There would be fun activities and a loving time. And then, one day I would go to bed but, when I woke up, he would be gone. So, obviously, I grew up loving the extra closeness and fun times but dreading the loss I would have to face the next day.

The repeated pattern of closeness followed by loss has become one of the scenarios that I had to control in my life as it was too painful to endure. As soon as I felt really close to a new boyfriend my alarm bells would start ringing. I knew how to deal with the loss but I could not bear the waiting for it to happen — that was far too painful. It became clear that I was manipulating the situation so that it did happen; the relationship finished. In other words it, it became a habit for me to try to control how a relationship would progress. It was a complete 'survival' instinct that I developed.

The peculiar thing was that I never thought that I was the person responsible for my breakups. It seems I became so skilled in manipulating the events that I could even fool myself!

Until I went to Oxford I was not aware that I could not recall very many events of my early life; the memories that belonged to the times when I was younger than about seven years old were only few. Until then, if asked about my childhood, I would have said it was a wild, carefree and lovely one. I did not know that there were times when I felt sad and lonely, and possibly not wanted either. They were all buried in the depths of my subconscious.

Years later, after I had developed my communication skills, this was also confirmed by the Spirit. In January 2003, I had a visit from an uncle whom I'd never met. He died aged sixteen when my father was still at the university. The only thing I knew about him was that in my father's score book, there was a small piece of music dedicated to him. It was named 'Sick Child' with two dates scribbled next to it. The first date showed the date my father composed the piece for him and the second date, which was only two months later, showed the date of his passing.

My uncle communicated with me after the passing of my mother's brother, another uncle whom I was very fond of, confirming his 'safe arrival'. Part of this conversation was about my childhood.

He said that when I was young, I was turned into an angry child. Being left behind often by my parents, I shed lots of tears and could never get used to it. He then told me that the anger had been the driving force behind me throughout my life; however, it was now changing, and slowly being replaced with love.

13- BECOMING A SPIRITUAL HEALER

The London Spiritual Mission used to hold a Healing Clinic twice a week and occasionally I would go to receive healing. One of their healers was a friend of mine. She was also a spiritual medium. It was sometime in 2003 when I went for healing for the first time.

The Healing Clinic was set up above the Library where we also had the Closed Circle meetings on Tuesday evenings. On this floor, the main room opened into two tiny rooms where we could receive healing privately. I lay down on the bed in one of these rooms, and my friend commenced the process by holding her hands around my head, then moving down to my body. She was not touching me but holding her hands about ten centimetres away. I closed my eyes and tried to relax. Soon, I had the sensation that she rested her hands gently on my head, and I simply allowed myself to really relax. In a short while I heard her moving down until she was standing at my feet.

Suddenly I became aware of the sensation of her hands being both on my feet and my head at the same time, and realised that she could not possibly reach both ends of my body from where she was standing! Reluctantly, I opened my eyes. There she was, at the end of the bed, and I could see that both her hands were across my ankles. It was amazing to find out that she was given assistance! I must admit it was only after that experience that I started taking healing really seriously.

In my Closed Circle, there was an elderly lady called Pat. For some reason, she would never say she connected with Spirit. When it was her turn to tell the group about her experience, she would smile and say she saw colours. One of the girls in the group would give her a lift in her car every week. One evening, she turned up without Pat, and said she had waited for her but Pat did not come to the arranged meeting place.

The following week, we found out why she was absent. The evening before the previous meeting, Pat had suffered a brain haemorrhage and was at the Charing Cross Hospital in intensive care. We were also told that the hospital would not give information to anyone outside the family. We were all very sorry for her.

The next day, I first contacted Pat's oldest daughter and explained who I was. I then asked her if the family would allow us to call the hospital for permission to go and give her mother healing. She was very pleased for me to go ahead. I called the hospital and I talked to the nurse in charge, explaining to him that we are a group of Pat's friends and would like to come and give her some healing if possible. He said he could not see any harm in that and asked us to come to the intensive care after 8.00 pm in the evening, when the ward would be quieter. Three of us from the Closed Circle went to the hospital the next evening.

Pat was in bed in a busy room of eight patients, most of them comatose, with the nurses quietly rushing around. We found out that Pat had undergone brain surgery a few days earlier, and she was still in a coma. She looked asleep and peaceful. We sat next to her and the nurses drew a curtain around us. At the time, only one of us was qualified and working as a healer. I had no idea what I was expected to do but felt strongly that we could help. We all tried to give healing to her in the ways we felt appropriate. I simply went quiet, and into a meditative mind, held my hands over her body, and asked for healing. When we all felt we had finished, we left.

I called the hospital the day after to check on her. I was told that she had been taken out of intensive care! Of course, there is no way we could claim any credit for it, but nevertheless we were very pleased. I followed Pat's recovery through her daughter; when I would call and ask for news, she would say; "Oh, you are the spiritual lady," which was nice to hear!

My next involvement in any kind of healing followed soon after — during one of my visits to Istanbul in early 2004. Two of my young friends asked if I could teach them meditation. I was more than happy to share all I was involved in and learning myself.

We arranged for my friend and her husband to come and pick me up. We would then go their friend's flat where three more people would join us. When my friends arrived, I noticed that the husband, who was driving, appeared to be in some pain, his shoulders were pulled up, and he was crunching over the wheel. His wife explained to me that he had been suffering from a spasm in his back and shoulders for the last three weeks, and though he'd seen two doctors, and received an injection, he had not felt any relief.

We arrived at their friend's house and were waiting for another person to turn up when I suggested that, maybe, I could put my hands over his shoulders. I do not know why I said it at the time, all I know is that I was just suddenly inspired to offer. Given permission, I put my both hands over his shoulders for a few minutes. I then felt that my right hand was not really required to be in touch, so I continued to lay my left hand and lower arm on his shoulders for another five minutes until I felt that I could stop. By that time, the other person also arrived and we started our meditation. Once we finished, they all asked if I would be willing to give messages to them from their loved ones in spirit. Again, most enthusiastically, I agreed.

My friend's husband was a civil policeman and 42 years of age at the time. He did not want to take part in spirit communication, and said he was going to the kitchen to have a cigarette. I had two communicators who gave their messages to those in the room — but the third one, I felt, was for the husband. So we invited him back from the kitchen.

He was not a very happy man to be asked to join us again! He did not like moving around as he feared the pain would get worse but agreed to come back to hear what was on offer! He sat down on the edge of the sofa with his shoulders so hunched they were almost around his ears. I proceeded with the description of a lady who appeared to be not a family member but someone close to the family. Soon after I started describing the communicator — a woman — tears started coming down his cheeks. He told us that she is his Aunt Emel, who lived next door when he was very young. His mother would leave him with her if he was too ill to go to school, and his mother had to go out. Aunt Emel would look after him. He was obviously taken aback by the evidential information given to him. He then asked me if she was touching him!

In my mind's eye, I saw her putting her left arm along his spine, a few centimetres away from his body, with her hand held over the back of his neck. The gap between her arm and his body seemed to be filled in with a white substance, which appeared to be sticky, not completely solid, and with no straight edges. It appeared almost like a very dense fog. Somehow, I knew that it was ectoplasm and told him that she was giving him healing. Ectoplasm was not something I knew much about or had seen previously myself. I had only seen it in some very old photographs taken at a Victorian physical seance and I never came across in the context of healing.

His aunt Emel also had some suggestions about how and where he should sleep, and others, which I passed on. As she withdrew, he stood up for a few seconds, and then his shoulders dropped. He looked to his right and then left, and said he didn't feel as if he had anything wrong with him! It was my turn to be shocked. I sat there with my mouth open, as did the rest of the group.

As soon as I was back in London, I went to see Terry Tasker, the Healing Secretary at Spiritual Association of Great Britain. I told him the story and asked what was I supposed to do. He answered, "Well, you do not need to do anything, you are already channelling healing. However, if you want to call yourself a Healer, you should do a course to be qualified as a Spiritual Healer, and get insurance cover." I first contacted Spiritual Association of Great Britain and then The College of Psychic Studies. I inquired about the healing courses they offered but it was already too late to join to either of them, their courses having started some time before. I then contacted the Corinthian Healers. Although they did not have a course planned to start soon, they offered to provide a teacher if I would be able to bring a group of people together. So, I contacted the friends I met at my development circle to see if they were interested. Most of them said they would be very happy to join me.

My flat was situated most conveniently to everyone, and so we had the classes there. As we were already spiritual mediums, it took us much less than a year to qualify, which made us all very happy. In March 2005, we all became Spiritual Healers accredited to the Corinthian Church and Healing Association (CCHA) and could obtain insurance cover for future healing work.

I believe such miracles, as happened in Istanbul, do happen but I do not believe healing necessarily happened because 'curing' him physically was the priority at that time. I am told by my guides that life cannot be extended or cut short even by a minute; we will pass into spirit when it is the given time. Healing given may be for the patient to cope and even progress emotionally or spiritually. As miraculous the healing in Istanbul was, I believe the reason it happened was to encourage both me and my friend's husband to start recognising our own gifts. He had previously told me that he would sometimes see faces on the wall while just sitting in his living room, but when that happened, he felt scared and refused to go along with it. I believe he was sensitive and the miraculous healing was given to him as a sign that there was nothing to be frightened of. What he had experienced was a gift that he should start taking seriously. It was a wake-up call in the nicest possible way for both of us!

My understanding and development as a spiritual healer had been a slow process. Looking back, it is interesting to see how each experience contributed to my understanding. The messages I received along the way encouraged me to persevere, to be open to learning further, and to allow guidance both in the spiritual healing work and how it contributes to find meaning in our lives.

In January 2005, I was in Istanbul and, once again, I joined my friends who had introduced me to the Spirit in 1987. The communication was with Avicenna along with some of their relatives and later the Virgin Mary! This time my spiritual development was confirmed:

> *"Esi is opening, her light is shining more and more, she needs further perseverance."*

I was also advised

> *"never to judge people"*

and was told that

> *"by not doing so will take you much and much further".*

We had a short break during our seance when I was inspired to do a portrait of a man. I could also see him in my mind's eye on horseback, riding over vast plains with mountains in the distance. He wore a turban on his head. I wondered if it was the portrait of Avicenna. I did not say it out loud but questioned it in my mind. Once we went back to the circle, the first message given was

"Yes, it was me!"

I now had a portrait of Avicenna which is reproduced at the beginning of the book. What I did not know at the time was that he would later become one of my Healing Guides! At this session, I was informed by him that I have healing gifts. Another interesting thing he said was that when giving healing, one should not wear shoes with rubber soles!

The last conversation we had was with the Virgin Mary who spent the last years of her life in Eufesus[4], in Asia Minor (now Turkey). As the communication went on, I inquired quietly in my mind whether I could do a drawing of her. The answer was given through Kayhan, saying:

"Virgin Mary does not give pictures"!

Here are some of the notes taken from the conversation with Avicenna:

> *"Death is very pleasant experience. Don't forget, life is eternal. All the material possessions are worthless. Once you are here, you are surprised. Do not hurt anybody".*

> *"Esi has opened up. Her soul is shining but needs a little bit more effort. The blinds are not fully open yet!".*

> *"Esi, do not judge people, be open. Everyone is at a different stage of their spiritual development. Never judge. You will then rise much further".*

---

[4] (http://en.wikipedia.org/wiki/House_of_the_Virgin_Mary#Discovery_in_Turkey)

(Referring to my friend who was pregnant at the time.)

"Always think positively. Consume hazelnut, walnut and banana. Red meat is not good. Eat as much fish as you can. The Phosphors are essential for a baby. The brain is 'woven' in the mother's womb".

"Esi, you are in contact with different channels, best to clean up. Listen to your soul. You are receiving messages almost like a postman. Sometimes you go back to old bad moulds. Anger, resentment, not giving a helping hand to those in need. To judge and scorn are the biggest sins. Once you stop, you will be amazed".

"Esi also has a healing gift. Once you listen to my advice, it will grow stronger. Try not to wear shoes with rubber soles when giving healing".

(Any suggestion with regard to my previous thyroid cancer?)

"Do not worry as long as you keep your vibrations positive. All the illnesses are caused by repeated jealousy, animosity".

"Esi your soul is reaching us here. Not everyone can. You are all mature souls. The physical 'beauty' is not valid here. We see the spirit as a source of light".

(Any advice on reading books on the subject?)

"Investigate first. Ignore the acrobats with words. You are receiving strength from your father".

"Souls like you all should gather more often. You give energy to each other".

(Addressing my friend again.)

"Listen to your soul, that is where the answers are. Do not see people with negative energies. They take your energy".

(Addressing the problems that my friend's husband was having at the time.)

> *"It is a gift from God. Fear, doubt, not trusting closes the door. Must be positive".*

(Last advice for me?)

> *"Keep to my advice. All support will be given".*

> *"From now on, watch your steps. You are chosen ones. There will a big cleaning up in the world but you won't be harmed. The difference is not in the 'bodies' but the 'spirits'."*

After returning to London, we continued with the healing classes. The healing teacher also was a medium and sometimes he would link to his guides at the end of the session to give us messages relating to our development. I received another message, which was that it is not the first time I have been involved in Spiritual work; in my previous lives I also worked for Spirit. But, this time I 'took the bull by the horns'. I was also told that I have an American Indian guide by the name of Vataka who is also working with me, and that he has been with me since I was a child.

A short while ago, in one of my deep meditations, I saw in my mind's eye an American Indian man on horseback on the top of a high hill with a sharp drop, surrounded by a barren land. His posture was such that I knew he was a very dignified man and he conveyed the feeling that he was very proud of me. So strong was the feeling that it brought tears to my eyes.

Following that I made a portrait of an American Indian man. It was, therefore, exciting to be given a message that confirmed him as one of my guides.

36- Vataka (Drawn 28.6.2005)

The Spirit helps us to heal in many different ways. In fact, we all are healers and give healing to others in our daily lives when we sit down and listen to them. It can be as simple as that. As Avicenna said in August 2008:

It is this Civilisation which makes you sick.

You have made your own voice a weapon, an enemy.

Only if you knew your strength, if you knew how to open your heart, if you knew how to listen to the sound of your breath —love is the medicine.

Today, I am grateful for my own emotional experiences as they enabled me to have empathy with a much larger group of people than would otherwise have been the case, with both my spiritual work as a medium and healer, and as a clinical hypnotherapist (which was another interest I would develop and become active in few years later).

The value of my psychotherapies was underlined by a message from Avicenna when giving healing to a distant cousin of mine in my early days as a healer in 2006.

One of my cousins and his wife are architects and, at the time, they were living with their teenaged son. They had always been an extremely close family. His sister told me that he had undergone gall bladder surgery a year earlier and ever since had been suffering on and off from a very high temperature. It had become so difficult that he stopped working completely. His doctors had not been able to find out what was wrong with him.

I had not seen the family for some time. His sister, who knew that I was now qualified as a spiritual healer, suggested that maybe I could visit them in their flat in Istanbul. So I did.

The following is the message I received as I laid my hands on him:

> *"In order to get better, he needs to reclaim his power. He should start an emotional journey.*
>
> *"He took on himself all he believed as his duty. Emotions he has considered as weaknesses. Emotions are the road signs. His energy has been consumed on the happiness of his family.*
>
> *"The illness was not sudden. It was the depletion of his energies. The duty is a life-style, carried out only when required. To own it makes you depleted.*
>
> *"Ask him to keep a pen and paper by his bed, and open his own heart to himself. He should write whenever he wakes up through out the night.*
>
> *"Happiness is finding your way back to your soul. He should open his eyes to the window of his soul. Ask him to feel his own soul, and be grateful. I am taking over from you, we will look after him. Provided he wants it.*
>
> *"It is with love that soul opens up, and it is nourished with love. Don't ever say that life is short. Until the time you open*

your wings and join us, life is not a duty, it is journey for your soul.

"Dear Esi, you opened Fahri's heart, let us fill it with love. He should claim his power. What we want is not duty but opening his way. The love is the signpost. His lesson was to learn emotions, to open his heart to himself.

"Be with love."

14- HEALING MESSAGES

Communication with loved ones in Spirit is sometimes the only healing a person needs. I include some stories below, which illustrate. In these, the communicators not only showed to their loved ones that life is eternal and that they are sill alive and supporting them, but also provided them with information that ended some of their sufferings from guilt and shame.

THE DECEASED FATHER GIVES
COMFORT TO HIS DAUGHTER

The portrait below was drawn during a private session with a small group of people at a friend's house in August 2005. My friend, whose house we gathered in, is also a medium and we wanted to experiment working together, so she invited a group of her friends over. It did not turn out to be as useful an exercise for my friend as she had hoped: all invited were close friends, and she therefore found it difficult to trust that the information she received was from Spirit and not derived from her own knowledge!

As for me, I enjoyed the session. I did several drawings and passed on the messages. I remember this one especially as it was another first as far as my experience went. As soon as the face below appeared on the paper, one of the women said she knew whose picture it was.

37- Peter B. year of birth not known— 2004 (Drawn 6.8.2005)

The person who was communicating made me aware that he had put on a lot of weight towards the end of his life. So much so that I felt each time he sat in a car, the car would sink a little! This was accepted and confirmed. Further evidential information was also given, and accepted by the recipient.

He then said: "He was taken by the loved ones." I repeated this out loud and asked if the person was her father and taken to the hospital by some people from his family. She accepted that he was her father but rejected that he was taken to the hospital by someone from the family. The father insisted, saying, "He was surrounded by the loved ones." This was again denied.

I left it at that as I could not change what I was being told. At the end of the afternoon, the lady came over to collect the drawing. She was almost in tears.

She apologised for not accepting some of the information earlier on and expressed her gratitude for the messages. She then explained that her father lived alone, and was given lots of medication, one of which was Cortisone. That is why he had gained a lot of weight towards the end of his life. She would visit him every Saturday, and take him out for his weekly shopping. Each time he sat in the car, the car would sink a little!

The week he died, she had been extremely busy at work. She had not been able to visit him on Saturday that week, or any other day of the week before he died. She, therefore, had terrible feelings of guilt, berating herself that she let him die alone. When I mentioned that he had "loved ones" with him, she could not initially accept it as she knew he had been on his own. However, thinking about it, she realised what he was talking about.

He came through to let her know that he was not alone when he passed into spirit but was helped by the loved ones in Spirit! He wanted her to feel no guilt about it. She said it was very comforting to know.

HEALING THE SHAME

In the summer of 2010, I held demonstrations in Hong Kong and Istanbul. This was my first visit to Hong Kong since I had lived there (I left in1999) and also the first visit to do any spiritual work. While living there, I was aware that there was a growing interest in spiritual and psychic work although I was too busy with professional activities to be involved. I was, however, surprised to find out that I was the first visiting medium to demonstrate spirit portraits.

In Hong Kong, I did quite a few demonstrations and interesting private sittings but there was one sitting that had a very surprising outcome!

A Chinese lady came for a sitting, hoping to communicate with her beloved father who had died when she was a teenager. Her father indeed came through and provided plenty of evidence about his character, profession, clothes, etc. All of these were accepted except for one detail — the details of his passing.

The father made me feel as though I was falling into a deep sleep, slumping over the chair. This experience was repeated four or five times, but each time I expressed this to her, the lady shook her head and said "No." She finally revealed details of his passing. Apparently, her father had committed suicide, having tragically jumped to his death from a cliff.

We left it at that but all that evening something was bothering me. I ended up calling her the next day, asking if there were any witnesses to his suicide. Her answer was negative. With the information provided by her father, we came to the conclusion that it was possible that he did not commit suicide; instead he could have just tipped over due to dizziness or from having consumed too much alcohol. There could be many reasons. In the end, these possibilities were a great comfort to her. It seems that her father did not want her and her mother to suffer any longer from the shame of a suicide in the family.

THE COMFORTING MESSAGE WITH A DRAWING

In October 2010, I did an interesting private sitting for a female paediatrician. She came to a workshop I had given few days earlier. During the workshop, she mentioned that she was grieving over the death of her child.

As we settled down and began the sitting, my mobile phone rang. Annoyed with myself, and embarrassed that I had forgotten to switch it off, I simply glanced over to see who was calling and immediately switched it off. It was a close friend.

I first sketched a portrait of a lady and continued with the description of the person. All of a sudden I was urged to do another drawing.

This one was a portrait of a young child who had bandages wrapped around his head. I asked the sitter if she recognised the child. Could it be her child? Was it a patient?

She did not recognise the drawing. I asked her to keep the portrait. This could be a reminder of the past, or of what was to come. Later on, I switched on my mobile phone and noticed that my friend had left me a voice message. She was crying and screaming, and was asking for my immediate help. I traced her to a hospital. The story actually was revealed in the emergency room.

My friend had taken her mother, her five-year-old daughter, and her two-month-old son to the park that evening. As they were leaving, they came across some iron steps up from the park to the street level. A man offered to give some assistance in lifting the pram, but as he did so, the two-month-old slipped out and fell onto the metal step. They immediately took him to the hospital where it was determined that his skull was fractured and that there was a possibility of internal bleeding.

It suddenly dawned on me: why had I been given a portrait of a boy whose head was wrapped in bandages around that time. The child I 'saw' had a mischievous grin on his face. The message to me was clear! I told my friend that everything would be all right. We were all relieved when it was reported by the doctors that child was indeed healthy and there was no neurological damage.

The next day, when I called the paediatrician she was amazed to hear the story behind the child's portrait. It took me few days to receive it back from her. I was even more surprised to see that the drawing was not of a young child but a young man. It seemed like another clear sign that the child would grow up to be a healthy young man. This is another great example of how Spirit helps us to cope with our lives.

The post script to the story is even more interesting: when I last visited Istanbul in October 2015, I met the mother and the boy, who is now five years old and a rather active and cheeky child. His mother gave me his photograph, which had been taken only weeks before. The portrait drawn when he was only two months old has an amazing resemblance to him at the age of five.

38- The boy with bandages around his head (Drawn 4.8.2010)

A MESSAGE OF FORGIVENESS

More recently at Barnes Healing Church, it was a rather full service and all the portraits drawn were claimed. Usually, the portraits drawn are for different people, occasionally two being claimed by the same person. In this occasion, three portraits were accepted by the same young woman. She later explained that she had been to a Spiritualist Church only once before, saying, "it was ages ago." She had not seen a spirit artist working before, and considered herself new to Spiritualist ideas. So, she was overjoyed with the messages and the drawings she received.

The drawings had similar physical characteristics common to all of them, and she could accept all the names given as well. The young woman later explained that her family was from India. As I recall, the first portrait was of her mother who used to wear lots of jewellery, the second portrait was of her grandmother who was a very bossy woman. The final drawing was of her father, and the message from him left her in tears. "Remember, you are my daughter, keep your chin up."

She later told me her story. She fell in love and wanted to get married but her father opposed the marriage, and refused even to discuss it. His last words to her were rather hurtful. "Next time she comes to him, it will be his corpse!" And she had not seen him since. She said it was very comforting to have him communicating and in his own way saying that he still loves her and is with her.

15- CONFIRMATION OF HEALING SENT

With spiritual healing, there may not immediate signs of healing except relief from pain and quick improvements in physical symptoms. Spiritual healing is usually met with suspicion and is questioned in the mind of the person at the receiving end. It happened with me when I started going for spiritual healing. Even though I already had sufficient evidence showing me that we do not die but live on in another dimension, I was not sure about Spirit healing!

With my training for spirit communication, the evidence is most important and must be provided; how else could I trust the communication? With spiritual healing, I could not help but question it as well. The first question that would come to my mind was whether the person giving the healing was indeed a channel. The second was whether I was really receiving any healing. Today, I am lucky enough to link to their energy and check if the person giving me healing has the gift, and who is helping them in spirit as they put their hands on me.

I usually give healing to a person present in the same room with me, but sometimes I am also contacted for distant healing. In this case, I am not necessarily sure whether the healing was received or indeed if it was for the right person. The following story is about distant healing and how I was pleasantly surprised with the evidence provided.

DISTANT HEALING DELIVERS GOOD NEWS

A lady called me from Germany and told to me she had been suffering for some time from a physical pain in her hips, which made sleeping difficult for her, as well as a skin condition on her hands. The initial treatment given by her GP and a physiotherapist did not help much, and further investigations more recently carried out were rather vague. However, they pointed to the possibility of cancer. She was feeling worried about an upcoming appointment for a CT Scan which would lead to a final diagnosis.

We had few days before the appointment, so I asked her to sit somewhere quietly for a short while, and meditate at an agreed time for the next few evenings. I explained to her how to breathe and relax. On the first two evenings, I felt that my hands were moving as if she was sitting in front of me, trying to assess what was wrong with her. It was on the third night that I received a message that not only informed me that she did not have cancer, but also gave some additional information. Initially I thought the additional information provided was pointing to the cause of the problem. I was most amazed and pleased when I received her reply.

I include her letter to me below, which explains:

"S. Platch- Munich, Germany (Nov. 28, 2010)

"The pain from which I was suffering since May 2009 did not improve with the physiotherapy and the acupuncture treatments I received. In fact, the pain continued to increase.

"I then had a MR scan performed on 16 September 2009 and I was confused by the result. The radiologist had sent a report to my GP saying that he suspected bone metastases. I immediately requested a full body PET CT scan but the earliest appointment could only be given for the following week.

"The same evening I called Esi to share my confusion with her and asked her if she could help me with the pain. She told me to sit in a quiet room at 11 o'clock at night for the next few days and that she would be sending me distant healing. The very first session was impressive and for the first time in weeks I had much less pain and slept peacefully.

"Esi continued sending me distant healing for the next few days. She then sent a message saying her guides informed her that there is metal in my body. She suggested that I have it investigated, perhaps by having a strand of my hair analysed. She was also told that I should not worry because my illness is not what I was told.

"I was surprised by her message. I told her that I was involved in a traffic accident when I was young and I now have a metal

plate and screws on my scalp. The other news of not having the suspected metastases on my bones uplifted my spirits but, as strongly suggested by Esi, I still went ahead with the medical investigations.

"Esi kept in contact until the appointment date for the PET CT scan and I had much less pain during this time. The test result showed that I did not have cancer and my pain was due to some infection in my bones.

"It has been over a year since I received the distant healing from Esi. My pain, although much less, is still continuing regardless of the medical treatment I have been given. It is only recently that I found out about Esi's web page and wanted to contribute my own experience to it. I now plan to visit her in London and hope to have some contact healing."

I was really happy. What we were given was some evidential information to show that the healing had been sent to the right person!

HEALING FROM A MOTHER

At Stockwell Spiritualist Church in June 2010 two portraits turned out to be of people still alive. I had been guided to do the drawings of living people before, but neither at a public demonstration nor a Spiritualist service.

In fact, this was the first time in a Spiritualist Church that two of the portraits drawn were of people still alive, and the communications made were for reasons different from any other previous demonstrations I had given.

The first portrait was of a male shown as middle aged. I then received more information about him but, when I passed it on, a young woman said, "I know this person, but he is still alive!"

That was a complete surprise to me. It was only then I became aware that there was a different communicator with me. Next to me, standing by me, was an elderly woman whom I described and her description was also accepted. The communicator then said, "I am his mother and I came through to give healing to my son."

The young woman who accepted the communication, later came to collect the drawing, and explained to me that the reason she came to the church that evening was in fact to put the name of the man in the portrait on the distant healing list, which she had done, as soon as she arrived. He was, in fact, her mother's partner, and elderly. He very recently had an operation and was still at the hospital, therefore, he was in need of healing!

It was wonderful to have it confirmed that he was receiving healing without me knowing anything about him, and that he was receiving it from his own mother! The other interesting thing was that his portrait showed him as middle aged, rather than elderly as her mother last saw him!

WHEN CONVICTION IS NEEDED!

The same evening a second sketch was drawn; this time it was the portrait of a woman. A man sitting in the congregation said he recognised her. He also accepted the further verbal information given relating to the person in the drawing.

At the end of the evening, when he came to collect the drawing, I found out who she was. He said she is his neighbour who has been unwell for some time.

He had met her the previous Wednesday and suggested that she may like to come to the church on Sunday to receive some healing after the service. He said she just shrugged her shoulders and replied "You would never see me in a Spiritualist church."

We both hoped that she would now have sufficient reason to reconsider her decision.

HELP ARRANGED IN ADVANCE

Here is a story that still amazes me in the way a meeting for an emotional healing was set up by the Spirit. It also demonstrates that there really is no coincidence in our lives. The Spirit does reach people not only to provide them with evidence that there is no death and that life is eternal, but also to pass on healing messages, which they did not know they needed!

I was invited to Ankara, Turkey, for a demonstration that would be recorded as part of a documentary commissioned by the Turkish Radio and Television Corporation. The documentary was called *At the Edge of Science* and it was planned to consist of seven one-hour episodes. The documentary maker contacted me in London. She explained that she wanted to make a film about various fields of research that push the boundaries of science and inquired if I would be interested giving her an interview about my spiritual work, my communication with the Spirit, and the portraits the Spirit does through me.

At first I was reluctant as I had seen some other UK documentaries on mediumship and did not think the subject matter had been treated fairly or seriously enough. There is usually an unfortunate tendency to turn it into a spooky entertainment. At the time, the woman in question did not seem to have much experience or knowledge on the subject either. I tried to encourage her to do some research and familiarise herself first. I also insisted that the episode I would be part of would have to be sent to me for my approval before it could be broadcast. All was eventually agreed and after several telephone conversations and correspondence, the film crew arrived in London.

I arranged for the crew to visit two Spiritualist Churches and interview other mediums and spiritual healers. They also filmed a demonstration by another medium. As for my demonstration, I suggested that we arrange it to take place in Turkey so there would be no need to translate. Moreover, as there are no Spiritualist churches or centres in Turkey, it would be a first-time experience for most, if not all, of their audience, and therefore it would be much easier for them to understand and appreciate in the Turkish language.

My visit to Ankara was arranged for January 2013. I did a demonstration of Spirit Art, which was filmed. After my demonstration, I stayed on for a couple of days so that those wishing could book private sittings and therapies with me through the centre where the filming took place. The private sittings would be booked for an hour, and the hypnotherapy or past life regression sessions for up to two hours.

On the second day, a young woman arrived and she said she had lost her young child but she was not interested in any kind of spirit communication. She came to see me because she wanted to experience any of her past lives. I checked the time allocated for the booking and had to inform her that her booking was for only an hour, which may not be sufficient for what she wanted to experience. As I already had another booking after her, I suggested that we go ahead with Spirit communication. She could let me know in the next ten minutes if she was not happy with the information and we would stop. Otherwise, we would have to cancel the session altogether. She agreed.

The session turned out to be rather interesting. The young woman wanted us to continue so we did. There were two portraits drawn. The first one was of a young girl aged about four or five, wearing a coat with small collars and a hat decorated with a large ribbon tied in a bow. The child I was seeing was holding a pencil and drawing quick crude lines on a piece of paper which suggested that she was feeling very frustrated and angry. The young lady said the drawing reminded her of her own mother when she was young. Her mother had pictures showing her dressed in a similar coat and with a similar hairstyle. There was also mention of a goat!

The second drawing was of an elderly lady wearing glasses with her hair tied back in a bun. The young woman again said the drawing reminded her of the family pictures of her mother. I then inquired who the communicator was and the person who came through was her grandfather. His message to her mother was profound apologies. I asked the lady if it was possible to pass all this information to her mother. She said it was possible and that she would, but was not sure whether she should do it on the phone or fly over to where her mother lives and do it in person. We left it there.

The next day I returned to Istanbul. It was couple of days later when I received this call from the mother. She confirmed that she could accept all the information and the drawings made. The drawing of the young child was of her, and the lady was not her mother but someone who looked after her as a child and to whom she felt as close. She also said she would be willing to accept her father's apologies. As for the goat, she said they had a goat around that time and she had adopted it as a friend. It was later sacrificed, which upset her immensely.

She then inquired if we could meet and talk face to face. I explained that I was in Istanbul for only another few days and asked where she lived. At the time, my mother was still alive and I could not accept bookings at her place. I said that Istanbul is a large city and it may not be possible to arrange a meeting. I was most amused by her answer: it turned out that she lived only a ten-minute walk from my mother!

We arranged for me to visit her. She was a very pleasant woman and was excited about the portraits drawn and the messages sent to her. She later told me that she had been having panic attacks for some time and would be interested in seeing me for hypnotherapy on my next visit to Istanbul.

16- HEALING THE SPIRIT

Having had cancer, I know how frightening it can be, especially if it reaches an advanced stage. When I had cancer in 1981, it was not even a 'C' word. That may sound flippant, but the seriousness underneath the joke is that cancer was unmentionable — almost taboo. I was a young architect and urban designer trying to gain experience and find myself a place in the professional world. I was living alone in London and had no family close by. It was a terribly lonely time, made even worse by people refusing even to talk about my condition.

In the early investigation stages, I would try to bring the subject up with friends, saying, "I may have cancer" in order to start a conversation and, maybe, share my feelings about it. But all they could offer was "of course not" as a way to reassure me, but though well meant, it was not really comforting!

I can now see that they simply did not know what they could say. They probably felt helpless themselves. They did not appreciate that all I needed was someone to listen to me. I have been advocating since that it is a subject to be discussed and talked about openly among the family or with friends, even though there may be no answers one can give.

Today, I also advocate Healing as the best 'support' system — as it should not necessarily be taken as the healing of the physical body. Years ago, my guides gave me the message that our lifespans cannot be shortened or extended by us. However, what we can do, I firmly believe, is help people to heal emotionally or spiritually even when physical healing is no longer possible.

We should never underestimate how much our loved ones in spirit can help us both emotionally and physically.

MOTHER'S HELP FOR HER SON

One interesting and moving experience that shows the value of emotional support from spiritual healing while receiving medical treatment was one I was privileged to experience with an old friend.

In November 2005, I heard that an old friend, Cengiz, whom I had not seen for several years, was receiving treatment for kidney cancer. He was an architect and, as far as I knew, spent most of his life living alone in the UK. Before I moved to Borneo, he met another architect friend of mine at a picnic I organised and I later heard that they had married. I did not know anything about his family or previous relationships. I was told that he'd already had an operation about six months before and started receiving chemotherapy after that.

They lived close to me, so I arranged to visit them. As we were sitting and talking, I started telling them about my new interest in spiritual work and the recent experiments I had been part of within my development circle. I was hoping that my friends, who were usually somewhat cynical, would at least listen because what I was telling them were my own experiences rather than hearsay stories about other people. I spoke of some of the evidence I'd received from loved ones and how surprised I was myself. My intention was to encourage Cengiz to start questioning whether there really is such a thing as death or whether life is indeed eternal, and that by thinking about these ideas, he might be able to face his illness more easily.

I then offered to demonstrate and see if I could communicate with anyone for them. I immediately had two women communicating: Cengiz's mother and his aunt. I repeated the information I received from them about the house where he was brought up. The information I received was mostly visual, so I could describe the rooms, the house and some other details. The aunt lived nearby and had no children of her own. I also felt that Cengiz's father was a very busy man who had not been around much while he was growing up. They all shared a house for their summer holidays and as a result of all these factors, Cengiz was brought up as a single child with the help of the aunt.

My friends seemed to be impressed with the accuracy of the details about a house of which I knew nothing. There were some other memories also given and lots of uplifting messages. In the process of writing this book, I met with my friend's wife again to go through my notes and ask her to confirm that they were correct. In the event, she not only did that but also reminded me few other messages.

One of the messages she helped me to recall was interesting. Again, it was given as a visual image at the time. In this scene, his mother and aunt laid him down and covered his whole body with the leaves of some kind of plant. We could not make much sense of it except that they seemed to be wanting to ease the pain and discomfort he was feeling. Later on, another friend to whom they mentioned it offered an explanation. Apparently, the friend's grandmother also used the leaves of the willow tree in a similar fashion when they were young and not feeling well. She told them that it was widely used in folk medicine and that extracts of the leaves are used as one of the main ingredients of aspirin today!

A week later, when I called them to check how he was, I was told that Cengiz had not been eating for the past few days. His wife was so worried that she attempted to have him admitted to the Royal Free Hospital by ambulance, but that there were delays and an ambulance's swift arrival was not guaranteed. Apparently, when I heard that, I offered to take them in my car. I also gave him some healing. Following the healing, while waiting in the hospital for a doctor, Cengiz requested his first meal in a long time, which surprised them all.

My friend stayed in the Royal Free Hospital for about six weeks while receiving treatment. He was back home for the New Year and was then transferred to the Royal Marsden Hospital early in January 2006. I visited him often during his stay in the hospital. Each time, I offered to give him healing and he gratefully accepted. On one of the first occasions, as I put my hands on, I received a message from his mother which I told only to his wife. His mother simply said, "My son will not have any pain, we are giving healing through your hands."

He did not respond to the treatment as well as hoped and was then taken to the Marie Curie Hospice in Hampstead at the end of January. He was there until his passing on 18 February 2006. During his stay, I visited him every day to continue giving healing. The incredible thing was that the promise given by his mother, which he knew nothing about, was kept. He did not have any pain and did not require painkillers until the day he died. He was supported by his mother and aunt, both physically and emotionally, during this very difficult time.

He also had support from other members of his family in spirit. Once, sitting next to my friend, I saw an old man with white hair and a long beard, dressed in white, arriving in my mind's eye. I instantly knew that he was a very respected religious man, so much so that when he entered the room, other people would stand up. He approached my friend, followed by a young man similarly dressed. They did not speak. The old man stood there for a few seconds, nodded his head slowly, turned around and left. I described this scene to my friend. When Cengiz heard this, he told me something I had not known before. His great grandfather was Semsi Baba (1795-1884) who in 1865 established the Order of the Lodge of Bektashi (one of many Islamic Sufi orders) in Yaghaneler, Izmir, Turkey. To this day, followers visit his tomb. We can only assume that the pious man I had seen and described was Semsi Baba.

Following the old man's visit, I would sometimes hear the most beautiful 'divine' music being played as I gave healing.

The following is a message I received from Cengiz's mother about two weeks before his passing:

> *"The last few days of my son. You never failed to visit him even though you were busy with your work. Please give my love. Please don't forget that we also went through what you are going through now.*
>
> *"It used to scare us to depart from the earthly home too. It was the others we were mostly concerned for. As is the case with my son, we also found it difficult to leave.*
>
> *"The light of your home is so bright that it dazzles us on this side. Your development with the love of your soul has become the voice from our heart. We will support his faith until the last moment. All the sedatives needed is passed on from your hands. As you can see, there is no other medication for it.*
>
> *"We can not soothe the pain our daughter is feeling but she should know that there is no death, what ends is the material. With death a light is switched on. We do know that the sadness*

in this foreign land will not dissolve in a day. She will be supported by her parents in our world and her daughter in your world.

"Keep lightness in your heart. Do not think that all of these and the sorrow you are suffering from in this foreign land is for punishment; see it as a game. As is with the hard times, days with joy are also an illusion. The important thing is the lessons you learn. The best is not to fight with life. We are supporting our son until his last moments.

"Death is not a mystery, it is a door into the light. Prior to his leaving his flat, you already shown him that death is not a separation. He was not willing to leave but now he appreciates every moment of his life, he is fully contented prior to his departure."

On the evening of 18 February 2006, I stayed in the hospice with Cengiz and his wife as I felt that his passing was imminent. My friend's passing was peaceful.

His wife told me "He was the kind of person who loved life and was very scared of death. Towards the end, he firmly believed in life being eternal and his passing was therefore peaceful."

This was confirmed by a message from Avicenna:

"It is not 'hope' that you give to your friend, it is the 'faith'."

When I asked what is the difference? The answer was:

"Meaning."

I believe his message was to say that my friend was starting to see life' in a new light and this experience would bring 'meaning' into his own life.

The next day, I inquired from my guides whether they had any news from him. I was told that he was met by his mother and his aunt and her husband. He saw them when he opened his eyes. I then asked when he opened his eyes and was told:

> *"It is not his physical eyes in the sense you use to 'see', it is his soul's eyes. He 'saw' when he opened up into his spirit. He stayed with you, watching. He was laughing and crying as you all did so."*

17- HEALING CHILDREN

I believe my own childhood experiences enabled me to have empathy with many children, both alive and in spirit. I know that we do not necessarily need to have been subjected to physical or verbal abuse to be hurt. However, the following story puzzled me at the time. Going through my notes, I came across the following message from Avicenna.

> *"Loss of health is not a punishment, it simply is a cry for help for the energies that should have been supporting your body but are spent on something else, therefore, your body is suffering. You need to re-claim your energies back."*

The healing stories of two young children, below, opened up a new understanding for me. In both cases, the children to whom I was asked to give healing were very young. It appeared that their doctors had no clear explanations for their illnesses. It also seemed unlikely that their illnesses could have been caused by any emotional scars in their own lives as they were far too young to have lived through much. The answers were given by the Spirit, even though their stories are still to unravel in time!

A TWO-AND-A-HALF-YEAR-OLD PATIENT

I was invited by a friend to a party given to celebrate her daughter's ninth birthday. My friend had previously inquired from me whether I could be of any help to her neighbour's two-and-a-half-year-old daughter and asked me to join them that afternoon.

I was told that the child was suffering from an auto-immune disease, one of the manifestations of which is a particularly low blood platelet count. The parents were told that the exact cause is not known but that the disease usually affects children and the main symptom is excessive bruising. At the time, she was being treated with Cortisone. The parents had been warned by the consultant that the girl's spleen may need to be removed at the age of six if there had been no improvement by then.

The treatment given, and the possibility of the little patient's requiring surgery, sounded rather drastic to my friend. She asked for my help. I could not refuse even though I had no idea of the kind of help I might be able to give. It was the first time I had been asked to give healing to a young child. So I went to the party, at least to offer some comforting words to the mother and to try putting my hands on the child.

Little Nisa was a very active child, and she refused to sit still, even on her mother's lap, so I could put my hands on her. I was of course a stranger to her, and she was really too young to be interested in any stories I could offer. I observed her, and she was very much like any other child of her age. Before I left, I suggested to her mother that she calls me once Nisa falls into sleep later in the evening. I told her that we may be required to do the same for a few evenings, and I would pass on to them any information I may receive from the Spirit.

The mother called me just after 10 pm. I then meditated and sent her distant healing. Just before I finished, I received a message asking me to inquire from the parents whether the child was in contact with her paternal grandmother. So I called them, and the answer was "Yes, on Sundays." Soon after, the mother called back to clarify: "actually she is not her real grandmother but her grandfather's second wife."

It turned out that the grandparents were separated when Nisa's father was only eighteen months old. His father remarried and did not allow the first wife to see her son. The mother moved to another town, and the two had not seen one another again until recently. It was only then that the real grandmother started visiting them during the week. The grandfather was not aware of this. Nisa, her father, and her grandmother seemed to be getting along well. I inquired if they ever discussed why she had been absent for so long, but it seemed to be a subject neither volunteered to bring up.

On the second night, they again let me know when the little girl was asleep and I sent her distant healing. This time I was asked by my guide to inquire if the child slept in the same room as her parents. I called to ask, and the answer was that she did. The mother said that they wanted to be near her if and when she woke up. As the issue was brought up, I asked if there was any possibility that she may sleep in another room, suggesting that they leave the door open so they could hear her if she woke up. They agreed, and told me that they had also been playing for some time with the idea that she should have her own bedroom, but that they had not been organised enough to buy a new bed for her. They assured me that they would attend to it as soon as possible.

On the third day, I travelled to a coastal town in the south of Turkey for a short holiday, but managed to sit and send her distant healing after the child was asleep. I received no further messages. The following night, I called to ask if they had managed to separate the bedrooms. The answer was "no." I told them that when I returned to Istanbul, I would like to visit and put my hands on the little girl while she slept.

Soon after I returned to Istanbul, I visited their flat one evening. I was pleasantly surprised that the little one had her own bedroom, nicely decorated, and that she was asleep in her new bed. I put my hands on her gently. After a short while, I received a message confirming that she was going to be fine!

I left, passing them the message I was given. We agreed to keep in touch in the future.

This story showed me that children are vulnerable to the emotional turmoil of the adults around them. The help and the messages given to me by the Spirit indicated that the illness of the little girl was the expression of her energies not being able to support her fully within the existing circumstances. I hope to follow the story of little Nisa and I wonder if her father will be brave enough to face his own emotions one day.

NO EMOTIONAL BASE

One of my previous healing clients, called DI, contacted me. Her best friend's son, a year and a half old at the time, had been diagnosed with Duchenne Muscular Dystrophy (DMD). The parents were told that the illness is a genetic disorder with no known cure. It is characterised by progressive muscle degeneration. Sufferers are expected to be using a wheelchair before the age of 10 years, and life expectancy is short — usually not beyond the teenage years.

DI was calling to inquire whether I might be able to help them. As usual, I told her that could not possibly promise any help, but would be happy to give distant healing. I asked them to let me know when the baby was asleep. In my first healing sitting, I was asked to make arrangements for another healing session by my guide. The following evening, after my distant healing session, I was informed that:

> *"The cause of the illness is not emotional. The family does not seem to have any other members who suffered from the same illness in previous generations. The parents seem to have a positive attitude to life. They should not accept it as the final word and should not impose it as such on the child.*

> *"The illness may have happened for various reasons and may improve in time. It seems that only the boy's legs show weakness at present. You may suggest to them to ask someone who can help with his legs to get stronger meanwhile. We can look into this again in near future should you wish."*

I passed the messages on to the parents. They confirmed that as far as they were aware, no other family member had suffered from this illness. And, yes, it was only the legs of the baby that appeared to be weak.

I was pleased to have my information confirmed. I appreciate how dreadful it must be for the parents when their child faces such a bleak future. I was, however, inspired to let them know about two real life stories I'd recently discovered. They are stories of two different families, in two different countries, who each raised a child with major physical disabilities.

I first came across the video of an interview with a young girl called Jennifer Bricker, who at nine years old was member of the 1996 American gymnastics gold medal team. She has no legs. She was abandoned at birth by her biological mother, and adopted and raised by another couple.

I found out about the second extraordinary person, a Turkish artist called Armagan Esref, when I watched a video interview with him. He was born in 1953 without sight, and he was about seven years old when he learned to paint using oil paints.

They both had shown the most amazing will to succeed regardless of their disabilities. But what also impressed me were the people who raised them, and how they instilled such will in their children when they were young. I asked DI to tell these stories to the parents, and to tell them to be positive. I said, of course, I would not even like to entertain the idea, but sometimes such disabilities or illnesses can be the biggest gift both for the child and the rest of the world.

18- ANIMAL HEALING

Since qualifying as a spiritual healer, I have attended a few animal-healing workshops. Having been an animal lover all my life, I always brought home and adopted cats or dogs until I moved to the UK. I would also have an army of strays outside to look after. My last two dogs in Istanbul were a Terrier and a golden Spaniel. Giving them away to friends was far too painful when I left for my studies in Oxford. I did not want to own another one until I knew that I settled down somewhere. So far, I still am required to do too much travelling to adopt one.

My interest in animal healing was triggered by a Spirit communication some time ago. I was at an afternoon demonstration at the SAGB's magnificent building in Belgrave Square in London. I cannot recall who the medium was. I was sitting at the beginning of a row, and following the communications the others were receiving.

Halfway through the session, the medium, pointing to the floor next to me, asked if I had ever owned a large German Shepherd dog. I was amazed. I did have a German Shepherd dog that I acquired from an Animal Sanctuary when I was living in Sydney many years ago. She was two years old and was an extremely intelligent dog. I called her Canim, which loosely translates as my beloved/my dear. The medium then said that the dog was there to protect me, and I had nothing to worry about, which brought tears to my eyes. I was very touched as I recalled an incident many years before when Canim showed me what a loyal and protective dog she was.

At the time of receiving this communication, I was carrying out a large refurbishment project on a four-storey Victorian building in Kentish Town. I had just received the Certificate of Completion from the Camden Planning Department, but the client suddenly started revisiting certain issues that he had previously agreed to. I had been rather concerned about them for the last few days. Here she was again, as if to reassure me that I was safe.

While living in Sydney, I was sharing a single storey house in Paddington with two others. All the bedrooms were located along a corridor that opened into a large living room. My bedroom was the furthest away from the living room. One day, I was upset about something I cannot now recall, and I was in my room, sitting on my bed, crying. I could hear Canim's footsteps going up and down the corridor, coming to the door of my room then going away again.

Feeling sorry for myself, I was not paying too much attention to her. I only realised what she was doing when she finally came in, jumped on the bed next to me, facing the door, as if waiting for something to happen. When the other two friends appeared at the door, she started growling and baring her teeth. She had brought them to the door of my room to make them aware that I was crying but would not allow them to come into the room. I was so touched that it made me cry even more!

I now know that she has been with me ever since her passing. I have also been aware that some of the other cats and dogs visit me. Luckily, for some reason, they take turns! At night, I can feel them jump on my bed and sleep next to me. Especially at those times if I am feeling sad and lonely, they would be lying on the bed next to me, making me aware that I am not on my own, and as if to tell me I am safe.

MY VERY FIRST CAT CLIENT

Not long after I did few animal-healing workshops, a friend invited me for lunch at her house at Canada Water in London. We had met and become friends while we were all living in Hong Kong. Her husband was an architect and after returning to London, they moved into this modern town house next to the River Thames. Having lost their cat a short while before, they then acquired a three-year-old cat called Harry. I was told that he was a rather anti-social cat! Harry had a traumatic background, having been passed from one owner to another when he was still very young and then coming to my friends when the marriage of his second owners came to an end.

Having heard that I had just completed an animal healing workshop, my friends asked me to show my animal healing skills! The new cat apparently had been losing weight. They had been concerned and had taken him to the vet who could not identify a problem but ran some blood tests.

When I arrived, the cat was not at home. The living/dining room was on the first floor with full-height glass windows overlooking a reservoir of water. As we finished our lunch, we heard the sound of the cat flap downstairs; Harry had arrived. In a leisurely fashion, he came upstairs and, ignoring us, went to sit by the window, looking outside. I stood up, walked over to him, kneeled down and stroked his head. He was not entirely happy with my interest and he showed that to me by flicking his ear as if to say "I'd rather you did not touch me!"

I whispered to him "I would like to give you some healing, if you'll allow me to." I then stood up and returned to my chair. To our astonishment, he followed me. My friend was sitting next to me. Harry first jumped onto her lap, then onto mine, and made himself comfortable. I put my hands on his back and gave him some healing. After about ten minutes, I said that he could leave when he'd had enough. Within a short time he stretched himself fully and left. Everyone was most impressed. So was I with my very first cat patient! It was later reported to me that Harry regained his appetite and calmed down a lot after a few months.

THE CAT WITH CANCER

Another opportunity for giving healing to a cat arose in Istanbul. At the beginning of a hypnotherapy session, a client mentioned that her cat was suffering from cancer. Her vet had suggested that the cat be put to sleep but my client could not bring herself to allow it to happen. She kept saying, "Yes, she lost lots of weight but she keeps going on. How can I?" I offered to visit and give healing to the cat. She was happy to accept it.

I visited her flat and met her cat. I was shocked to see how much weight the poor thing had lost. She was so skinny that she looked like a bag of bones. She could hardly stand. The cat sat by me and I put my hands on her. Immediately, I was overwhelmed with sadness. I immediately knew that the only reason the cat kept going was because she did not want to disappoint her owner. I gave the message to the young woman and suggested that she talk to her cat and agree that she would let her go if that is what the cat needs. Two days later she informed me that she did as I suggested. That night she went to bed with the cat lying next to her. In the morning, she found that the cat had passed into spirit while she was asleep.

19- A HEALING LESSON GIVEN TO ME

After my return to London, I saw an advertisement at the College of Psychic Studies, which was offering a series of courses on Anatomy and Physiology for healers and students. I found it interesting because I thought it could help me to understand people's problems when they come to me for healing. As a person who craves for more learning, I was seriously considering it when I heard.

"So you think you are the one giving healing?"

So, that was the end of that!

Looking back, another important guidance from Avicenna was given in October 2005. It was to guide me in my future work both in terms of understanding and making sense of my journey. It helped me in 'hearing' the pain behind the issues of those who came to see me — whether for healing or the hypnotherapy sessions that were to follow later. The message was:

"It is your emotions which lead you in your life. Your emotions are the meaning of the earthly life.

"They called me the Scientist. What is Science? It is the voice of your Spirit.

"The desolation had been your companion. We put it with you so you see, hear, and do not fight. You have advanced, advanced much. You are being prepared for your new life."

Once again, I just recorded it. It was quite a few years before I could knowingly put it into use. I had no idea that one day I was to become a Clinical Hypnotherapist.

PART 4

DOOR INTO THE SUBCONSCIOUS

In September 2004 I had a most interesting experience. A friend of mine in Istanbul was expecting a baby. She was telling me how the baby was very active in her womb, moving and kicking. Feeling curious, I put my hand on her belly and, as I was waiting for a movement, I suddenly had a vision. I could see an old man with a long white beard, who was wearing a long, dark-coloured gown and a turban of the sort worn by high-ranking men in the court of Ottoman Empire, standing by a cobblestone road. There were no pavements on either side. On the left hand side, I could see a stone building. The road sloped up to the roof level and ended up running along a very old cemetery. There were poplar trees on the boundary to the cemetery. I heard the words "the grave is inscribed".

The old man said, "You will come to visit. You have to walk through the churchyard but it is difficult to find it on your own. I will help you." He said he would draw the route and then we would find it. But then he said he would do that only when the time given has lapsed!

He then gave information about the baby my friend was carrying. He said:

> *"The baby was previously the Crown Prince."*

and I saw a young man, about 17 years old, galloping on a horse. He continued:

> *"He used to go on expeditions on horse back. He was lively and fearless. He is coming back to earth to develop further, by his own choice.*
>
> *"Life is the best school. They ask for the recipe for life. They say you are the reason. Do they ever ask the one from the Palace?*
>
> *"I sent him on an expedition. He came back wounded on his knee. They said he is still away, gave me his respects but failed to tell me that they cut his throat. I did not know the death of the Crown Prince."*

As he was talking, I saw a dagger, decorated with inlaid semi-precious stones.

> *"Who you have is my dear son who went on an expedition but was murdered. The year was 1674. He was the meaning of life for me. I did not know the truth. I never heard his voice again. I was left only with his name. What you are given is my son, he will fight no longer. Do not feel sad. What is coming is love. I am the guide. I am his guardian."*

The old man was smiling as he talked about the prince. He said, "he will be much liked" and announced that I also shared his life. The guardian to the prince stepped back, folded his arms and, referring to my friend, he said:

> *"He is now entrusted to you."*

and went quiet. I passed all the information to my friend. I, then, found myself in a spacious room with very high ceilings. A powerful looking man, wearing a long coat, was now standing in front of me. The collar of his coat was made from white fur with black spots, which reminded me of drawings I'd seen of Ottoman Sultans. I looked into his eyes and saw my father smiling back!

20- PAST LIVES

I was quite taken aback by this experience but still had no interest in the subject of reincarnation. Two of the few books I had read on the subject were *Many Lives, Many Masters* (1988) and *Messages From The Masters* (2000) by Brian L. Weiss[5].

I also had come across in newspapers and magazines occasional stories of children who would talk about their earlier families in another city or even a different country, where their present families had never visited before. I read them with interest over the years but that was all. I never pursued the subject any further until I had to take part in an exercise during a workshop in Herne Bay given by Jennifer Mackenzie.

We were a group of about fifteen people in a spiritual mediumship development workshop. There was a mother and her daughter aged around seventeen in the group. While we were doing individual communication exercises, the young girl became quite emotional. Jennifer suggested that she needed a past-life regression as she thought the reasons behind her emotional state could be related to a past-life experience.

I watched them with interest but could not make much sense of it. Jennifer then asked if anyone else would like to experience their own past lives. They all did. She made a sweeping statement, which was difficult to believe at first. She said we would all be related to each other at a time and place, and should be able to regress to our shared lives. So she invited two people at a time to sit together, holding hands and regressed them to their past lives.

I still could not comprehend what was going on. They all seemed to have regressed, and were talking about lives lived long time ago — although not always shared lives. If it was shared lives, they would take turns to tell us their story; if not, they would then talk about their

---

[5]   Brian L. Weiss M.D., graduate of Columbia University and Yale Medical School. He was the former Chairman of Psychiatry at Mount Sinai Medical Centre. I found the case studies in his books most interesting.

individual lives. Up until that point, I had not volunteered and I was not willing to go through with it; it all looked a bit silly to me! However, at the end, there was only me and one other person left, and she was really keen to experiment. Not wanting to disappoint her by refusing, I unwillingly agreed to join in.

I was blown away by my own experience. It was like watching myself going through the emotions of an earlier life experience with all the sounds, smells, and other sensory perceptions such as the feel of fabrics and so on. It was the feeling of being present both now and in another time and place.

I knew that I was in England, sitting in a horse-drawn carriage, wearing a long woollen blue skirt. I could hear the sound of the horses' hooves striking the ground and feel the breeze in my hair. I was being taken to the family country house. I was young — in my early twenties — and very pretty. I knew that we were a wealthy family and from a noble class. We also had a town house and I would spend much time travelling between them. I had a dashing young father in uniform but my mother was nowhere to be seen.

I saw myself arriving at the country house, entering a big hall with a round staircase leading upstairs and quite a few housemaids standing by the door to welcome me. I was holding my chin high and not talking to any of the servants. I remember my present self being critical of my behaviour and my former self replying "that is the way my father wants me to behave!"

I was then regressed forward to an older age. This time, I was sitting by the window in the town house and feeling very lonely. I no longer had my father with me. It felt as if I was left on my own with no siblings, no relatives, no friends.

I seem to have had regrets about being extremely aloof and not talking to the servants. And when I was brought back, tears were running down my face. It was then that I became aware of the similarities between some of the experiences I've had in this lifetime and those from the past life just recalled.

In my present life, I have travelled extensively, constantly on the move from one place to another. I had a handsome and charming father whom I loved and who passed into spirit when he was 76 years old. Although my mother lived until she was 92, she had not been available to me emotionally — neither in my childhood nor later. I was away, living in another country, when I finally figured out the missing parts in my childhood: my yearning for emotional closeness with my family.

In my thirties, following my psychotherapies, I tried to raise the subject with my mother but she was very defensive. So I just let it be. After my father's passing, she lost all interest in life and was in a very long period of mourning that led to dementia. For the last fifteen years of her life, she had to be looked after. It seems in this life my solution was to make my friends my family.

This first past-life experience I've described was later followed by others and I have had the most incredible recalls of several past lives, each one giving me more insight into the repeating patterns in my present live.

And again, none of these were started intentionally in the sense that I consciously decided to look into my other past lives. In the spring of 2003, a group of friends from my Closed Circle decided to meet once a week to meditate. We would sit quietly and meditate for about 40 minutes. Whoever came out of the meditation first would gently bring the others back when the time was up. We put no conditions on how to go about it and gave no guidance except that one of us would do the opening prayer and ask for protection. All we had to do was allow ourselves to go as deep as possible. We could then share our experiences if we wished.

Geographically, past lives I recalled took place all over, from the United States of America, to Italy, to South Africa. One of the most strongly felt past-life experiences was in Africa, in the bush.

A group of us, some sitting, some standing, were watching the sun setting on this large flat land, empty but for a few large rocks and the shrubs of the bushland. I was sitting on the ground and could see two people standing further away to my right, both naked, and one holding something that looked like a wooden shield in front of him. It was very quiet, and it seemed as if everyone was awestruck by the scene. We watched the huge reddish sun sinking beyond the horizon. And suddenly, I was overwhelmed by feelings of nostalgia and a deep longing to be there. It was a feeling that I have never ever felt for any other place in my whole life!

In each past-life recall, the experiences were so very real, even as I stood by and watched myself, as I had done in Hong Kong, seeing myself crying and saying "that is what sadness is." The most striking aspect was that each lifetime had a 'topic' to experience and to learn from, and these kept repeating, albeit every time in different context: country, race, sex, age, and so on. In my own recalls of past lives, and those of any of my clients, this also seemed to be the case, so much so that once the past-life regression was over, we all seemed to recognise the common threads — and identify the repeating patterns — in our present lives.

PART 5

CLINICAL HYPNOTHERAPY

I was soon being approached by friends who wanted to experience their past lives. But beyond that, it seemed that word was spreading and others started contacting me too. While all of these experiments seemed to be successful, in the end I decided that it would be best to do a course in past-life regression and become properly qualified to perform such work. However, I could not find a course on past-life regression only; one had to qualify as a Clinical Hypnotherapist. At that stage, even though I was not sure how wise it was to get yet another qualification, I went ahead with it.

By the end of the course in 2009, I was extremely pleased that I had completed it and still amazed at how the knowledge and the experience I gained complemented my understanding of life on earth as a spiritual medium and healer. As a clinical hypnotherapist, I have been privileged to have such brave clients who shared their lives with me and who, in the process of my helping them, taught me a great amount. As clinical hypnotherapists we can help people who want to lose weight, or who have phobias or dependency on alcohol, cigarettes, etc., provided they want to do something about it. However, only a few people came to me because they wanted to lose weight. Looking back, I find it fascinating that most of the clients who came to see me had been carrying some form of emotional scar for a long time.

These clients either met me at a spiritualist demonstration, and found out that I was also a clinical hypnotherapist, or they came through word of mouth. What impressed me was the role my spirit communication demonstrations played. It seemed that thinking about the possibility that life may be eternal gave them the impetus to start questioning the meaning of their lives, no longer easily accepting that they had just been 'handed' a tough life.

They all felt compelled to tell me their frustrations about the anger, sadness, worries, doubt, or confusion in their daily lives, and sometimes we would notice recurring patterns of behaviour. Along with that, they started appreciating that it is sometimes certain aspects of themselves, or certain parts of their lives, that they have ignored or failed to see the significance of. With those clients, we always found the answers lay in their early emotional history, just as I had discovered for myself.

As a clinical hypnotherapist, I keep going back to the simple models developed by Eric Berne.[6] He based his theory on the assumption that all men and women have a multi-faceted nature to their personalities: the child, the parent and the adult, all existing simultaneously. Berne also accepted that past feelings and events stay locked together in our subconscious. Berne's theories have helped me and my clients untangle forgotten or confused earlier experiences.

Upon first meeting with clients, I ask them to complete a questionnaire about their life story and the history of the problem they have come to see me about. It is an important part of the therapy. As much as I learn about them, I would like them to feel that I 'heard' and 'understood' them as well. Throughout the therapy, I know that they

---

[6] Founder of Transactional Analysis as the basis for his psychotherapies in the early 1950s.

will guide me where it most matters to them and, most importantly, we will get the answers when they start hearing their own voices.

The little poem below was written by my father and I found out about it only recently.

You stand on this earth with child's feet.

The flying birds, the green of the trees

>*you see with your child's eye.*

The sound of waves blasting on the rocks

>*you hear with your child's ears.*

Then you read a story.

That is when you change.

Your ability to think, your power to design,

>*and your joy for life take the stage.*

And you start performing your tomorrows.

21- SOME LIFE STORIES

It is difficult to talk about some of the therapy sessions if those stories are divorced from the clients' life stories because their emotional pain is always so intricately woven into their earlier lives. I find that it is my own emotional experiences that now give me an insight into, and understanding of, the journey of others through their lives.

Following are some of these life stories.

BACK IN THE WOMB

An attractive woman in her thirties made an appointment to see me. She had previously been to some of my spirit communication and portrait demonstrations in Istanbul, during which she received some communication from a deceased family member. She wanted to find out whether hypnotherapy sessions would help her in trying to find answers to some on-going conflicts within her family.

She was living with her husband and their young daughter. This was her second marriage. In her first marriage, she wanted to have children but they failed to start a family. They divorced and she met a man who fell in love with her. She liked him. He was handsome and single. According to her, she felt that this could be a good opportunity to start a family. They started dating, she became pregnant and they got married.

She came to see me because after three years of marriage she was finding it increasingly difficult to live with her husband because of his controlling nature. He seemed to be blaming her for everything at every opportunity. She found it difficult to challenge him and ended up acquiescing. She was now beginning to question what it was that attracted her to him and why she could not say "No".

Her life history indicated that the answers to her questions could be accessed by an age-regression therapy. She was easily regressed, but to my surprise, she immediately went back to the time she was in mother's womb. She could hear her parents arguing. Her father's voice was loud and forceful; her mother's was anxious and crying. As an unborn baby, she felt threatened and scared.

She then went back to the time when she was two years old and her mother was pregnant with her brother. Her parents were again arguing and she, as a young child, felt frightened and insecure.

The few therapy sessions not only revealed her earlier family memories, but helped her to realise that the man she had chosen to have a family with was very much like her own father. By choosing someone so similar, she was simply 'protecting' herself by repeating the experience of a relationship she had previously 'survived'. It was a scenario she knew well how to handle provided that she stayed within the familiar territory. What she did not know was living with someone who would not demand her constant submission. It would have been such an unknown lifestyle for her that she could not risk it. The experience gave her sufficient understanding and built enough confidence in her not go along with the same script any longer. Now that she knew, she could start taking risks and, in so doing, heal herself.

Equally importantly, remembering her childhood emotional experiences was showing her what her own daughter was now being subjected to in their family life. So, therapy was helping her to heal not only herself but also some of the possible emotional experiences being scripted for her daughter's life in the future.

She later sent me this short testimonial to include on my website:

> *"It is always far too soon to lose a loved one. It is far more painful especially if you did not know the circumstances in which the person you loved dearly lost his life. It was through Esi that the final moments of my dear cousin's life were revealed and this information made it easier for me to bear.*

> *"Esi changed my whole outlook on death and dying. I now know that we only shed the body while our spirit lives on. I also know through experience that they are with us when and if we need them.*

> *"Esi is a very special person in every way. Even more so with the work she is doing to spread this truth of survival. She provides communication with the people we thought we had lost forever.*

> *"Through her hypnotherapy and regression work, she is also helping and encouraging us all to accept responsibility for our own lives and face our fears, and fulfil our own potential."*

I.L.T. 28.2.2010

SAFE AS A PIECE OF STONE

I received a call from a 44-year-old woman named Rebecca in Germany. A friend of hers, an American woman living in Istanbul and a former client of mine, suggested that she contact me. She then wrote to me as follows:

> *"Basically, I am utterly stuck and have been forever. Something reasonably powerful or simply unknown to me is keeping me immobile and causing me a lot of stress. I have no clue as to what my outlet could be, what it is I should be doing, trying, working towards. It all seems pointless to me. I somehow cannot connect any activity with me."*

It was the beginning of 2013 and I was due to fly to Istanbul in April. We decided to meet there when she could arrange a ten-day visit for her and her husband. It would give them an opportunity to visit their friends as well. At the time, I was seeing people at a local centre, so a booking was arranged for her too.

At our meeting, she told me that she recently lost her work. About two years previously, she felt that she was failing miserably at work and seemed to be in conflict with everyone. This disturbed her a lot so she started seeing a psychotherapist, and continued for about eighteen months. She said that with the therapy it became clear that there is a 'disconnection'. She would seem to be very engaged in a situation but actually she was not there! She said "Except in the case of my husband, friends and parents, I am intellectually aware but the core of me is not present, I am not involved, I do not feel it and people do not notice."

It became apparent that she would be enthusiastic about everything and would become engaged, be committed and productive — often, in fact, doing much better than anyone else. However, she seemed incapable of allowing herself to be a team member. She explained "It would switch me off, thereby sabotaging myself. After realising this, it became just pointless. I cannot start anything new because what is the point?" So she left the company and, when the pressure lifted, she ended her psychotherapy sessions.

While under the effect of the stress, she felt she was using a huge amount of energy to keep herself from exploding. "It felt like a pressure cooker that must not go off, but must be controlled. Something bigger was in control." She also said that it felt as if she was able to "unblock" herself, but she feared that she would find herself to be completely average, with nothing special about her.

Later on, she found out that she was incredibly creative with her hands but still refused to expand her gifts into any group or team activities.

Rebecca was brought up in a family of four. On a number of occasions, her mother was in hospital for prolonged periods. The father looked after them all. He would come home after work, and then cook and feed her and her brother. The brother, who was five years older, had been rebelling against his parents and was regarded as a 'real problem for the family'. He had huge fights with the parents. Rebecca was always well behaved, made sure that she followed the rules and met the expectations, and never made an issue of anything. As she was growing up, she quickly learned how not to be a problem but, in the process, lost her own 'child's voice'.

We could manage only three sessions in ten days; two of them with age regression. I could see that putting her feelings into words and naming them was difficult for her. One of the most touching experiences she revisited during the regression sessions was when, as a little girl, she would lie in bed thinking that she was turning into stone. She would then notice that one of her fingers was moving, involuntarily, and would feel relief that maybe it was not working!

Before leaving Istanbul both she and her husband wanted to have a separate session of Spirit communication. One of the communicators was her grandfather. The evidence provided and the messages given seemed to open a new door for her. They left with the determination to start meditating.

We kept in touch from a distance. After a number of months, I asked if and how she felt the hypnotherapy had helped her. At the beginning, she said, she had spoken about a happy childhood, but soon found feelings of loneliness, sadness, and anger that she can now understand and accept.

After the hypnotherapy, she started seeing her mother and father in a different light. She now feels "the stone was finally cracked and some goodness and healing infused into these cracks." She can breathe better now but has not yet shed the coat. Hypnotherapy planted a seed but she feels she neglected to care since even though she continues with meditation.

Rebecca later sent me this letter:

"Dear Esi,

"As promised here my thoughts on what changed after my sessions with you.

"If there is anything I should explore further to help you, please let me know.

"I now understand that others are just like me. We are all influenced by our pasts, and of course held back by our regrets or pains. I received acknowledgement and deep understanding that whereas I am privileged in many, many ways, I really was hurt and it left scars, and I can still feel the old pain today.

"But at the same time I gained realisation that others are just the same as me; by no means am I unique or alone in this.

"So I do not walk around defending myself from injustices so much anymore, but rather see the little person behind the grown-up 'perpetrator' and feel some sort of kinship to him or her, feel sorry for them and move on knowing that I am one step in the right direction towards healing and peace.

"This gives me enormous comfort and self-confidence, compared to before.

"The session in which you connected with my grandfather complemented this experience. I now do not feel so alone. I firmly believe he actually did connect, as crazy as this sounds to myself at times. But he is here, and he does love me, I am NOT alone, I DO matter and it makes my heart sing.

"Writing these last words, I realise they really sum it up — compared to before, my heart now sings. At least, sometimes! And this gives me hope, faith, joy.

"What a beautiful gift. Thank you, Esi.

"Just beware — it makes me want to come back for more!! I certainly still have a way to go. Only now I know it is all possible and not as cold, hard, lonely, and hopeless as before.

"Love and kisses,

"Rebecca."

THE GAMES WE PLAY DOWN THE GENERATIONS

The following story illustrates how life stories are carried down the generations and the role our families play in bringing us up to become who we are. In other words, how they contribute to the development of our 'life scripts' and the 'roles we will play'. In this instance, the story was revealed with the help of a great grandmother in spirit!

39- Roberto F. 1943- 2015 (Drawn 25.5.2013)

This young Italian woman first came to a Spiritualist service in May 2013. She recognised one of the portraits as that of her uncle.

She later sent me a copy of the drawing and a photograph of her uncle with a testimonial, below. At the time, her uncle was alive but undergoing treatment for cancer.

> *"The first time I met Esi was during a demonstration at Clapham Spiritualist Church.*
>
> *"Esi had just started to draw the portrait of a man, and I immediately thought of my uncle (who) was still alive, but I preferred to wait for more information before I identified him as my uncle. Esi then finished the portrait defining the character of the man.*
>
> *"Everything matched the reality, but when Esi even said the name, Robert, I no longer had any doubt that I was witnessing one of the most touching, exciting, real and deep (experiences) of my life.*
>
> *"Esi then described the spirit that had led her to make that drawing, and unequivocally described my grandmother (my uncle's mother) and she also gave me the first two letters of her name.*

"The message that my grandmother wanted to give to her son was a message of apology for not having shown enough affection during her life, for imposing too many restrictions, and being distant.

"Another message was to reconsider and rethink about a decision taken, a message that had no strong meaning for me, but nevertheless it did have for my uncle when I talked to him.

"My family and I were simply enchanted by the accuracy and clarity of messages that were delivered to us. Knowing Esi was a wonderful gift and I thank her for helping us to remember us that our loved ones will never leave us.

"An incredible emotional experience. Thank you, A.F."

A month after this church service, she came to see me to discuss the possibility of having hypnotherapy with me. Her main complaint was about her unhappy relationship with food. We were soon to establish that her personal life affected the way she treated food: her frustrations in her relationships made her look for comfort with emotional eating. Going through her family history, she told me that her parents live together in Italy. She loved her father although they were not close. There was a history of verbal abuse by the father towards her mother who was a sweet but rather submissive person.

She had problems with her choices of partners as well. She seemed choose men who would also verbally abuse, and lie to her. She had an on-off relationship with her current boyfriend. Each time he came back, she could not say 'no' to him.

We started hypnotherapy sessions and, after they ended, we remained in touch, so that I could be made aware of the changes taking place in her life. About a year later, much had changed. She finally said 'no' to her boyfriend for the last time. She was now a much happier and healthier person. She no longer relied on food for comfort. She was dating another young man of whom she was really fond. She now had a regular job and was living in a house she liked.

Around that time, she again came to a Spiritualist service at which I was able to produce a portrait of her great-grandmother. I later received not only a copy of the drawing together with a photograph of the lady, but her life story as well.

> *"Last time (when) you gave me this portrait you described a woman a bit sad…very kind with old manners…you said that music and musicality was very important in her life. She was sending healing for someone in the family who is in need at this moment.*

> *"Well, I recognised my great grandmother V., who was born in 1889 and passed away around 1983…not sure. What we all know about her is that as a young woman she was in love with a musician, a famous composer called Riccardo L. At that time, however, he was not yet famous; he was poor and from a poor family. Her family introduced her to another man, who was rich and from a noble family, and although she was not in love with him, she decided to marry him.*

> *"We all know that she regretted her decision throughout her life. In fact, she was the first woman in T…. to get divorced in 1916.*

> *"She is sending healing to her grandson, my uncle Roberto, who is in need right now."*

40- Virginia de B. 1889- 1983 (Drawn 4.3.2014)

Having heard the life story of the great-grandmother who communicated with us, I was curious and inquired about the life stories of her mother's side of the family. My client later shared the stories of her grandmother and her mother with me as well.

Here is the rest of their story, starting with her grandmother, A.

"She was born in 1913 and was very attractive: tall, slim, blonde with blue eyes. She lived in the countryside near Rome.

"She fell in love with a soldier, a few years older, from Sicily. They were lovers; he was married and he never left his wife.

"A. became pregnant when she was about 24 years old, but this didn't make the soldier change his mind about leaving his marriage.

My grandmother A. gave birth to a beautiful baby girl, L., in 1939. This little girl was my mom. She raised her on her own in a small village, where single mothers were not well considered, especially around the 30s.

"The soldier kept visiting my grandmother A. for the first two to three years after my mom was born. Realising the difficulty that A. was having in raising her child, he even offered to take baby L. and raise her in his family in Sicily.

"My grandmother did not accept the offer.

"She was beautiful and though she had a lot of interest from men around her, not many were willing to accept her and her baby. Apart from one: a gentleman from a good family who was ready to marry her and call that little girl his daughter for the rest of his life. This man was V., (great grandmother) V.'s son.

"A. and V. were married and they had another son together, Roberto. (the one in the portrait). They lived comfortably in the centre of Rome and they ran a small company.

"Again, I don't think my grandmother A. was in love with him; she married him because she needed to. They never divorced, but both had other relationships outside the marriage; my grandfather V. died of a heart attack while visiting his lover one night.

"The story had always been a big secret: my grandmother A., just few months before she died in 1998, decided to tell my mom the truth....and she did....but then she passed away, leaving my mom with doubts and questions she could not ask anyone about.

"My mom grew up without knowing anything about her real father. She told me that she was loved and looked after, but she always had the feeling that she was treated differently to her brother Roberto.

"She remembers being witness to some awkward family discussions that she never quite understood. But, having been so insecure, timid and fearful, she never asked.

"My mom also told me that one of her first memories of her life is of a tall man wearing a long black coat who used to pick her up, but she was crying. I wonder if that is the memory of the soldier...."

As the stories started to unravel, it was amazing to see how the unhappy relationships of these women down four generations repeated until my client started questioning her own attitude towards men and decided to take charge of her life! I was very proud of her.

22- OUR CHOICES RESPECTED

I feel extremely privileged to be able to communicate with Spirit and be able to channel healing to those in need. I neither request nor expect to receive any messages from Spirit while giving healing. Similarly, I neither expect nor want to make any diagnosis. We, as spiritual healers, are not qualified to do so. I trust only that Spirit is with me and all the healing will be received where it is needed most. If and when I do receive any information regarding the health of the person, I pass it on but make a point of saying they must follow their medical doctors' instructions and never assume that spiritual healing is to replace the treatment they are already receiving or will be receiving. They should accept it only as an additional support.

In addition, I know that Spirit will respect the choices we make in our lives. As in all communications with them, they tell us only what we *need* to know, rather than *want* to know. As regards our health, they may point us in the right direction, so that we pay attention to the choices we are making in relation to our lives. They would make it known that we have to take responsibility for our own lives.

In my experience, whether through hands-on or distance healing, the only assessment I seem to be receiving from Spirit is whether the illness has an emotional cause or not. I may receive a message pointing out whether there is an emotional situation surrounding the person either at the time of illness or in the past. As I was told so many years ago, in my first meeting with Avicenna in 1987, our energies are closely related to our attitude to life. It is clear to me that our attitudes are formed by beliefs and values, whether personal or cultural, which are developed by our emotional experiences throughout our childhood.

Having gone through my own emotional journey, survived cancer, and learned through it all that life is eternal, it seems to me that I was guided to become a clinical hypnotherapist. I now know that such experiences may be an essential part of our journeys on earth.

Today, the medical world is finally opening up to the possibility that people have self-healing gifts. Over the last few years, I have been lucky enough to support several people with serious illnesses; for some of them as a spiritual healer and for others as a clinical hypnotherapist. I have been encouraging them to find their own healing gifts to help to heal themselves along with their conventional medical treatments.

The following story is of a patient who helped herself to heal, albeit with a little help from a loved one in spirit!

DAUGHTER IS PATIENT OF HER DECEASED FATHER

I met SRV, Turkish woman, in London some time ago. Occasionally, I would see her at social gatherings with friends but though the relationship was cordial and pleasant, we remained acquaintances only. The last time we met again was at a conference in 2013. At the end of the conference, the friend who initially introduced us mentioned that SRV had recently learned that she had breast cancer, which had already metastasised to her liver. I instinctively offered to put my hands on if she cared to call me even though I did not expect her to take up my offer, as she had never shown any interest in my spiritual work.

However, she called me soon after and came to see me with the other friend. Although it was a social visit, as the conversation centred on spirit communication, I offered to see if anyone was there for her. We were not disappointed. Her grandfather wanted to communicate! The description of him was accepted. I cannot recall the details but she later told me that her grandfather informed us that she would not need an operation. At the time, I did not know that her treatment protocol had not yet been fully decided. And that turned out to be the consultant's recommendation to her soon after: her treatment would begin with a course of chemotherapy, with surgery to be considered afterwards only if required.

SVR was understandably very concerned about her prospects for recovery. I promised her that once her treatment started, I would come and sit with her in the hospital. She was grateful for my offer and I was happy to do it. However, I did not want to encourage her to believe that my presence would make the treatment work. I therefore told her that I would not like her to rely on my being there as any sort of guarantee that her treatment would be effective, so that if, for any reason, I was unable to turn up, she should not fear an adverse consequence. My suggestion to her was that we start with hypnotherapy sessions to help her initiate her own healing powers to support her during the medical treatment she would undergo. She was happy with my suggestion.

Subsequently, she and her family came to a church service I was doing near their home. She brought along her daughter and son, as well as her sister and her husband. I remember that they received a communication from her grandmother and a portrait of her as well.

Soon after, she was given a programme of chemotherapy, which would require her to visit the hospital every three weeks. We also started her hypnotherapy sessions. I first taught her how to relax and meditate. Her hypnotherapy mainly concentrated on building her own confidence and initiating her own healing powers, which are inherent in all of us. I made audio recordings for her to listen to every day. I also joined her at the hospital for a couple of hours during her chemotherapy sessions, in the hope that I could help her to relax. What I did not expect was that her late father should join us as well!

The first time I went to sit with her in the hospital, I sensed that a man in a white doctor's coat, whom I felt was very much a gentleman, was standing nearby. He turned out to be her late father who, in fact, was the chief physician of internal diseases in one of the major National Health Teaching hospitals in Istanbul before his passing. He was standing by us in the manner of a visiting consultant who had come to see how his patient was doing! It was a lovely surprise. From then on, I would see him visiting each time I was with her in the hospital. Sometimes I would see him approaching us, walking down the corridor; other times I'd find him standing by her bed. He had a lovely sense of humour. One time he said, smiling, "You can dress, now" as if he'd just finished examining his patient for the day.

Meanwhile, the patient continued listening to the audios and meditating at home. The side effects of the chemotherapy were much milder than expected. At that stage, it was difficult to claim that her meditations and self-hypnosis were helping her; however, the following events seem to show that it was precisely the case.

Halfway through her chemotherapy a scan was scheduled, which would indicate how she was responding to the treatment. Two days before the appointment she called me to ask if I could send her some healing. She said she was restless and could not sleep. At the agreed time, I sat down quietly and asked for healing to be sent to her. What I did not expect was to see her father communicating with me. I saw him stretching his right arm forward and, with his index finger and thumb, he appeared to be picking at something. As he reached forward, there was a flash of light, and then both the light and the father disappeared.

I was intrigued. I described to SVR what I had seen, but did not offer my own interpretation of it, which was that he may have been indicating that the small metastases in her liver were no longer there!

The following day she went to her consultant's surgery to discuss the scan before the appointed time for the next chemotherapy at the hospital. When we met at the hospital, SVR smilingly announced that her consultant was most pleased with the results revealed by the scan. Not only was she responding the treatment much better than the consultant had expected, but also there was no longer any tumour of any size in her liver!

Soon after, her father joined us! I heard him saying "She is considering having an operation." I was surprised to hear him say that, in the light of the favourable test results. I turned to my friend and asked what her father was talking about. She explained that she had been assuming all along that she would have her breast removed, as a cousin of hers had, after the treatment. I did not comment further and we left it at that. Her father then said that we should be working together, which I passed on.

SVR continued with the course of chemotherapy, and I went to sit with her each time. Her last treatment was at the beginning of May 2014 and I was due to travel to Istanbul for a few weeks later that day. This time, when her father joined us again, he was not wearing his white coat. He was dressed smartly, though casually, in a turtleneck jumper as if to signal the end of her treatment! I passed on to SVR what I heard him saying, and she took notes:

No cutting, no sewing and no travel yet!

(Showing Esi a little plant in a pot) This plant is now growing and has given the first leaf.

Dote on this plant, look after it and give it your love.

She should take a pen and paper and write down her emotions. She should open her heart to herself.

She does not need to share it with her sister.

Love is the treasure. It is given when needed. She has given herself only in drops. She has given all to others but herself.

The sister should also protect herself and change herself.

She has to get to know herself.

We have been successful, she is not coming back to here again but she needs to learn to love herself.

Then SVR's notes continue "the father calls Esi his friend. He put a kiss at the top her head and said, 'see you when you get back'!"

I left her with the notes that day and travelled to Turkey. I knew that it would be some time before she received the final test results but the days passed and no news was forthcoming! I finally emailed her to ask how she was. I was first overjoyed to hear that no cancer cells were present in her tests, but equally disheartened with the rest of her news. She had decided to go ahead with her consultant's recommendation to have the mastectomy.

Her operation was scheduled for the end of July 2014. A few days earlier, SVR called me and asked me if I could communicate with her father to find out his opinion about the operation. I understand how tempting it is for someone to ask for advice from their loved one, especially one they know cares for them, but I also do not like to encourage people to try to avoid taking their own decisions.

I simply suggested that she ask her father herself as he would hear her, and assured her that he would find a way to make it known to her. She later informed me that she did ask him the question before she went to bed. The night before going into the hospital, she saw him in her dream. She received the answer from him, which was "You decide for yourself!"

As I write these pages, SVR called me to tell me about her latest test results, taken eleven months after her treatment. The tests showed no trace of cancer in her body.

I reproduce below a testimonial written by SVR, from which it is interesting to see her side of the story.

> *"I was introduced to Esi through a mutual friend a few years ago. I knew that she communicated with the Spirit but did not think much about the subject until I became seriously ill. Until my illness, I led what I considered to be a healthy life style.*
>
> *"Towards the end of 2013, I was diagnosed with breast cancer and was told that it had metastasised in the liver. The news was a shock for the whole family. It was around this time that I saw Esi at a conference. She offered to put her hands on me. Since that day, and over the course of the last year, Esi's healing hand continues to guide and protect me. I know that when Esi reads this she will tell me off and say that I fought my illness myself, but she was the one who gave me the will to succeed.*
>
> *"She worked with me throughout my illness. We had a series of hypnotherapy sessions, some of which were recorded as audios. I listened to these in the evenings to help boost my healing. They gave me the self belief, and an understanding of the strength within me, which I could tap into.*
>
> *"I also received communication from my beloved late father. Esi and my father were with me in all my chemotherapy sessions. His encouraging messages were all borne out by the good scan results.*
>
> *"Esi gave me the strength to fight and not to give up. Through her guidance I learnt that good health is three dimensional; the*

combination of physical, mental and spiritual. I look at life differently now; I try to live every day to the full, taking as much joy from each moment as possible. I have learnt the importance of meditation. The 10-15 minutes of tranquility and listening to my body enables me to be guided by my spirit. Most importantly I am learning to love myself.

"Through Esi I am able to feel closer to my loved ones who have departed over the years. My father is always with me. I feel his help and positive energy.

"As far as the cancer is concerned I have had all the necessary medical treatments. The latest tests show no trace of cancer in my body. In other words I am here for many more years to come. I have resumed my normal life, and gone back to work. But there is a difference between now and before: I enjoy life a lot more, I am happy and I am grateful.

"One warning: Esi can create dependency. You can miss her positivity and compassion. From time to time she can also alternate between being hard and soft.

"Dearest Esi —Thank goodness you are here, you lit up my life in my darkest hours. May the road you travel always be full of light.

REMEMBERING A LONG-LOST CHILDHOOD FOR HEALING

During a recent visit to Munich, Germany, I was asked whether I could be of any help to a woman in her late sixties, named Monica, who had breast cancer. She already knew about my Spiritual work and was interested to meet me. I could not refuse to see her as I know that even a caring ear or a soft touch can make lots of difference in anybody's life. However, I made it clear that I am not a miracle worker and was in Munich only for a limited time, so I would not be able to start any hypnotherapy sessions.

Monica and her husband lived in the outskirts of Munich, by a lake. I went to see them one early evening. They were an extremely charming couple. It was easy to recognise how much they loved nature and lived simply.

She told me her story. The cancer was in her left breast. As a young girl, she had been told by her gynaecologist that her breasts were not regular; there were a number of lumps but they were normal, and it was possible that during the menopause they may begin to disappear. Nevertheless, some four years previously breast cancer was diagnosed. She was treated with chemotherapy and had been in recession until recently.

Then, the tumour returned, this time described as stage four. She was given only months to live and while the doctors recommended surgery, Monica refused as she felt that if she went into hospital, she would die. Instead, she opted for a light chemotherapy. She was happy with that for three months but then began to feel that it was not working as well as she'd hoped. She began a further course of chemotherapy but, again, it was not efficacious. Her left arm is now damaged and her left hand doesn't function.

I asked if she does meditation and she said yes; in fact she began doing so 15 years before with a group of people who channel to a drum, and she still continues to do the same meditation.

I talked to her and her husband about spiritual healing and clinical hypnotherapy, explaining what it means and what is involved. I then offered to put my hands on her. I asked if her husband could sit with us, in case a message would be given, and it would be useful if he could take notes as I do not necessarily remember it all afterwards. In fact, I did receive a short message. I was asked to inquire from Monica about her mother!

So I did. She told me that her mother is still alive and she has a brother who is nine years younger. She doesn't know her father. For the first years of her life, her mother had to work, so Monica was looked after by her aunt, and her mother would visit them occasionally. When Monica was five years old, her mother married, and came to collect her with her new husband. Monica was not happy, and she couldn't get used to living with her mother. For Monica, the mother figure had been her aunt. She kept crying until she was brought back to her aunt. I asked how she felt at the time. She found it difficult to put the feelings into words, but said she felt sad, alone, withdrawn and that she cried a lot.

I felt deeply for her but I could not help her apart from giving the message I received, which pointed to a time when there were unresolved emotions relating to her mother. I told her too that if she thought about those specific times, maybe she would come to terms with the pain stored in her subconscious since childhood. The fact that she was well looked after by a loving aunt, and kept in contact with her mother, could all be explained and acceptable to a rational mind. However, it seemed that her pain had never been emotionally processed, which indicated to me that her energies, without her really knowing it, were being exhausted by 'keeping the hurt alive' and leaving her with insufficient energy to maintain a healthy body. Much to be discovered!

PART 6

THE MISSING LINK

"Yesterday, I was clever, so I wanted to change the world;
today, I am wise, so I want to change myself".
— Rumi (1207-1273)[7]

It was in November 2004 when I received the first indication that I would ultimately write a book. The message given was:

"We will turn your articles into a book. Your stories of Spirit are increasing. Just be patient and keep your heart open."

Until then, I had simply been keeping notes, though not at first with any particular reason in mind.

Later, in April 2005, when I inquired from Spirit "Am I to write a book?" the answer I received was:

---

[7]   Mystic Poet of Mevlevi Order. His name in Turkish is Celaleddin; in Persian Jalalu"l-Din Rumi.

"There already is lots of material for a book but what is required is that you find the flow without searching for it! Tomorrow is a sunny day. You are not in possession of your voice yet."

It seemed that the message from my father, which I gave in the Introduction, was to tell me that I had found my voice, and now could put my experiences and my understanding into a book. Experiences in my life and my recent work as a medium, spirit artist and clinical hypnotherapist, had given me a glimpse of what a simple, yet so sophisticated, system our lives are based on and why. And the knowledge I have gained along my journey through life brought me to the conclusion that we need to consider our lives within a new context.

My story is a human experience — I am neither a scientist nor a doctor — but as a layman, I have always been interested in learning about the findings of the latest scientific and medical research. It is heartening to see that the scientific and medical worlds are finally questioning their materialistic and mechanistic view of life, which kept anything to do with Spirit and what makes each of us unique as a person outside their domain. Lest I should create the impression that these changes in thinking are widespread and fast-moving, it is important to make clear that this is not the case. Progress is slow, and the scientists involved, while highly regarded and respected, are literally pioneers.

I had the good fortune to encounter the work of Rupert Sheldrake[8] as a result of my involvement in the documentary At *the Edge of Science*[8] in 2012. Sheldrake did his Ph.D. in Biochemistry at Cambridge (1967), and has long been carrying out research on developmental and cell biology. He was one of the scientists they arranged to interview while in London. As he lived nearby, I took them to meet him, and through his interview I learned about some of his recent books and research, which seems to have started a controversy among his peers. In *Morphic Resonance: The Nature of Formative Causation* (2009) he puts forward the

---

[8] I am told that the documentary has not yet been broadcast. However, I was sent a short extract in which I appear.

theory that nature itself has a memory. In *The Science Delusion* (2012), he argues that science should be set free from 'ten dogmas' it is built on.

It made my heart sing! There are many others whose research has brought them to 'the edge of science.' Another pioneer is cell biologist Bruce H. Lipton Ph.D., who performed ground-breaking stem-cell research at Stanford University and whose book *The Biology of Belief: Unleashing The Power of Consciousness, Matter and Miracles* (2005) shows that all the cells in our body are affected by our thoughts.

Today, digital technology has made it much easier to communicate worldwide and, as a result, more and more of these new views and research findings are being widely circulated and publicised. In many ways, I am happy that they open up lots of minds, mostly to the ancient wisdom that has been long forgotten, but there are many findings that are confined to their own individual fields and unfortunately not as widely disseminated or able to connect with the bigger picture.

Equally important is that so many theories are being turned into practical tools and promoted as 'self-development'. Some may indeed introduce us to new ways of viewing our lives; however, it is also sad that others are little more than money-making machines, with their over simplified guidelines in the name of 'self development', and end up preying on the vulnerable. Examples are those movements that suggest that we can simply visualise, and then ask the universe for, money, a job, a partner, or whatever, and have us believe that it will be given. I personally would find it offensive to be told this. Do we think we are tourists on earth, just wandering through life with no purpose other than a visit?

I do believe in learning, but not at the cost of spending our precious time trying to follow others' simplistic ideas when our own lives are designed for us to learn from. However simple our lives appear to be to us, they are so intricately woven that they provide us with rich life lessons — though only if we are willing to open our minds and hearts.

I now strongly feel that there is an essential link that the scientific and medical communities are missing in their inquiries which, if recognised, would help not only them but, also, all of us to bring 'meaning' into our lives.

I consider myself extremely fortunate for the ways in which my life has unfolded because my journey now enables me to put all the knowledge and insight I gained into a new context. I could not have attempted to put it together, had I only read about them in the self-help media that have recently become popular. Let me put my argument to you in the way that it was unravelled for me.

23- LIFE SCENARIOS

Looking back on my own life, it was in 1980s when I first became aware of how my emotional experiences formed, moulded and influenced the way I had been viewing the world around me as I grew up, and how I responded to the opportunities life offered to me. In a way, I slowly became aware of the 'life scenarios' I had developed as I was growing up, and the role my past emotional experiences played in the formulation of these scenarios.

24- THE SPIRIT

I was then introduced to the importance of 'spiritual values', and use of 'spiritual energy' in our daily life through Avicenna in 1987, but it was at the beginning of 2000 when I became fully aware that we all are Spirit. There is no 'them' and 'us' — except the physical bodies and the personalities we chose for this 'school on earth'.

While I was living and working as an independent consultant architect and urban designer in Hong Kong in the second half of the 1990s, I would watch Oprah Winfrey's television shows. It was on one of these that I discovered Gary Zukav, a Harvard graduate with a degree in International Relations and a recipient of the World Business Academy *Pathfinder Award* for his "Contribution to the Ongoing Evolution of Knowledge and Consciousness within the Global Business Community", and the *Einstein Award* from the Albert Einstein College of Medicine for his "Contributions to the Psychosocial Growth of Humanity." I was already in conversation with the Spirit at the time, but I could not yet relate his 'Soul' with the Spirit I was talking to.

In his book, *The Seat of the Soul* (1999), Zukav defines 'soul' as 'the part of you that existed before you were born and that will continue to exist after you die', he added that 'our earthly life on this most amazing planet is just a short episode.' In *The Heart of the Soul* (2001), written with Linda Francis, they discuss the importance of emotions in our lives and introduce ways of developing 'emotional awareness' for our spiritual growth.

At the time, I could draw parallels with the messages I received from Avicenna and recorded, but it was not until I seriously started my own development with the Spirit that I could understand the importance of it all. This realisation was anchored by the development of my own gifts of communication. During my development, all the evidence I was provided with was important, not only to those in mourning for whom I communicated, but to me as well. To start with, I was the first one that needed to be convinced that they were not the product of my wild imagination.

The specific descriptions of memories long gone, details of personalities, the sense of smell and other sensations conveyed to, and subsequently accepted by, people I have never met, was awe-inspiring and convinced me without any doubt not only that the Spirit world does exist and we are all Spirit, but also that the Spirit survives death, and is eternal. Our loved ones are not 'dead' but still 'alive'! Some of the many pieces of evidence given to me form a large part of this book.

25- ROAD SIGNS

My own emotional journey, a major cancer operation, and finally the messages I was passing on to people who opened their hearts to the possibility of eternal life, and the healing they received just by the messages given by their loved ones in Spirit, all started coming together.

My work with Spirit also brought in some 'miracle healing' episodes, which encouraged me to become a spiritual healer. My real understanding and development as a spiritual healer has been a slow process. Looking back, it is interesting to see how each experience contributed to my understanding. The messages I received along the way encouraged me to persevere, to be open for further learning, and to allow guidance in both the spiritual healing work and how it contributes to finding meaning in our lives.

Knowing that the Spirit is energy, and that we have to utilise this energy correctly if we want to be healthy, I learned that we already do have a built-in warning system: our emotions!

As Avicenna put it:

"Emotions are the road signs."

We generally do not know how to deal with emotions and are never taught. While we are growing up, we are not taught to acknowledge, accept, and use them as our road signs. However, we do learn how to control them. For example, it is a fact that most of us breathe improperly. As adults, we tend to take shallow breaths, which we hold in the chest rather than the abdomen. If you watch small children breathing, you will notice that they breathe deeply and that their abdomens rise and fall as they inhale and exhale.

As we grow up, we seem to shift our breathing to the chest. This is not a conscious decision for any of us, but it has been shown that shallow, chest breathing allows us to feel more in control of events taking place around us.

Physiologically, it speeds the heart rate and diverts blood to the muscles so we can 'run away' if we need to. Further, energy stored in the liver is converted into fuel, our body releases additional hormones such as adrenalin and cortisol, all of which enables us to react quickly to any emotional stress. In reality, our reactions are those which have become habitual, the much-tested reactions within the scenarios we have developed through our lives. While we 'think' that we are protecting ourselves, we are only reacting to stress and ignoring the real emotions — therefore, not only increasing the stress we live with, but also continuously releasing hormones that in the long term harm our immune system.

It was also in the late 1990s, while living in Hong Kong, that I discovered Caroline Myss, again through the *Oprah Winfrey Show*. In her book *Anatomy of the Spirit: The Seven Stages of Power and Healing* (1997), Myss writes about energy healing and how hidden stresses, beliefs and attitudes can cause illness. In *Why People Don't Heal and How they Can* (1998), she discusses 'how your biography becomes your biology.' This was the first time I had taken notice of energy centres called 'chakras' but they became a reality to me only when I 'saw' them myself in one of my healing development classes much later.

26- CHOOSING YOUR LIFE

I then had opportunities to experiment with past lives. The book *Many Lives, Many Masters* (1988) by Brian Weiss, M.D. was one of the first I read on the subject in the late 1990s. However, it was not until 2004 that I had my first experience of recalling one of my own past lives. More followed soon after.

The glimpses of the memories of my past lives I recalled, and the stories of others I witnessed, have convinced me that we reincarnate into this world more than once, and we do so in order to face certain challenges in different contexts. I was also told by the Spirit that we choose the context within which we reincarnate on each occasion: the country, the society, the family and even the time period in which to be born.

Thinking about Weiss's book, and comparing some of his cases to my own past-life experiences, or those of others in which I had first-hand involvement, I was surprised that none had translated directly to the healing of an illness or a psychological issue in this lifetime as he writes of. In our stories, what we discovered were the main 'themes' of our chosen challenges, and how and why they kept on repeating in different contexts. The only common thread in each case was that the lessons learned help in our spiritual understanding and growth rather than manifest in materialistic gains.

This led me to realise that we all have different roles to play in our society. We are on earth not only to develop as individual spirits but to play our roles for the others around us that we have chosen to be with — to facilitate their development. It is never one role and one answer!

27- CHILDHOOD

My experiments with past life memories were to lead me to qualifying as a clinical hypnotherapist. I had been directly interested in the idea that our minds consist of more than one component, and that our consciousness is layered. This theory is largely accepted by most psychologists and cognitive scientists. It is generally agreed that the part of the mind that we use in our daily lives accounts for about 10 percent of consciousness, and it is this part by which we manage our lives, make decisions, and direct our various activities. The remaining 90 percent of our consciousness is called the subconscious (some prefer the term 'unconscious'), which is used as a storage facility where all our experiences, since birth, reside.

During my training, it suddenly made sense to me that the consciousness we as adults use in our daily lives does not develop in children until the age of six or seven. Children are extremely vulnerable and dependent on others to take care of them. Without the benefit of any analytical thinking capability, they have no choice but to go through whatever their daily lives throws at them. Faced with situations that appear to be unfair, threatening, or scary to them, they cry — but this is not only for lack of language, it is because they cannot express or discuss the anger, injustice or anxiety rationally as we adults can.

What if the adults don't love them anymore, or simply put them outside the door? Who is to care for them? For children, survival is the only thing that matters. They need to feel safe and loved, and they also need to feel valuable. And so, we all develop survival patterns, test them each time we need them, and as time goes on, perfect them.

We become so skilled at manipulating that we even fool ourselves as we grow into adults.

Children's daily experiences are stored in their subconscious as sensory experiences. Those that are repeated later form our habits or, in some cases, phobias. Others might form the basis for our fears and anxieties and, depending on their severity, some we want to disown may even be buried deep in the subconscious, not to be remembered until a time when a new triggering event takes place.

As adults, because the experiences we had as children are sensory, in any new situation in which we find ourselves feeling uncomfortable, stressed or even challenged, these feelings may evoke our childhood experiences, even if not consciously remembered or related to, and these are expressed as emotions.

All of our childhood experiences stored without the critical, rational, analytical or thinking facility behind them, will form the base on which we build our outlook for our future life experiences. These determine our understanding, our attitudes, our expectations, and our beliefs about everything that is taking place around us. They will be the lenses through which we view the world.

In 2009, I was excited to discover Dr Bernie Siegel M.D. through his book *Love, Medicine and Miracles'* (1987). Now a retired paediatric surgeon, he was one of the pioneers who became aware of the role of emotions and taught his patients to take responsibility for their lives, empowering them to live fully.

I then discovered other pioneer doctors such as Dr C. Norman Shealy, M.D., PhD., a neurosurgeon and physician, who was instrumental in developing the American Holistic Medical Association (1978) and Dr Emmett Miller M.D., who played a role in creating the field of Mind-Body Medicine.

The importance and the role of emotions are finally gaining recognition in a wider medical and scientific world, and taking place on the main stage in relation to our general well being. Dr William Lee Cowden is another doctor — a cardiologist, nutritionist and internist in Integrative Medicine — who sees one of the causes of ill health as 'exhausted emotions' and the effect on our immune of emotional conflict and stress. He believes in the potential of healing ourselves.

More recently, clinical neuropsychologist Mario Martinez, after studying centenarians all over the world, found that cultural and spiritual beliefs are more significant than genetics when it comes to health and longevity and, on the basis of these findings, developed the theory of Biocognitive Science.

28- TRUSTING LIFE

A year or two ago, I was listening to an interview with a well-known American author who is also a spiritual medium. I found myself in agreement with most of his views, and thought he was wise. However, I was very disappointed when, referring to childhood memories, he defined them "as the poison that you were fed." It seems he completely missed the whole point of being a child and having childhood experiences. What he didn't seem to appreciate is that our childhood experiences shape us to become who we are until a time when we are ready to question our choices and experiences. That is when we start 'learning'.

I feel that our emotional childhood experiences, together with the obvious 'learning' from each lifetime experience, all fit the purpose, so eloquently expressed by Gary Zukov, of coming into this 'earth school' as a human being.

Let us accept the argument that we incarnate into this world for our development as spirits and that we choose our challenges in each incarnation.

In order to become the person who would be challenged by certain issues, we first need to be raised in an environment that will facilitate the necessary feelings of inadequacy, dependence, superiority (or whatever they need to be). It would then follow that it only makes sense that we *choose* the family — with both its emotional and physical attributes — country, race, time, etc., that we are born into. This 'environment' then, both in micro and macro scale, will provide the determining influences as we grow up to become the person to face these challenges.

These may turn us into a specific type of person — for example a 'controlling person', a 'pleaser', an 'avoider', a 'victim' — based on the behaviour patterns we adopted, and tested again and again through our childhood. These patterns of behaviour may equip us to deal with situations and enable us to survive, but when we are challenged and taken out of our comfort zone, we are faced with stress. While these survival patterns may not be themselves defined as problems, being under extended stress may lead to serious illnesses, psychological or behavioural problems. Only by becoming aware and starting to question, do we begin to learn from our own life experiences. *Reaching this awareness is the point at which we start taking responsibility for our own lives and trusting life.*

I believe that life always continues to offer us other opportunities — even when and if we keep repeating our 'mistakes'. We are always guided and supported by our loved ones in Spirit whether we are aware of their still being alive or not. They allow us to repeat our mistakes because they respect our choices; life, after all, is a series of choices.

Having read my stories of my spirit communication and seen the portraits drawn, I hope you have accepted that consciousness belongs to the Spirit. How else would those in Spirit, the so-called dead, provide those of us who have the gifts of communication with descriptions of their physical attributes, their personalities, or their shared memories so that they can be identified without any doubt. In other words, giving us 'evidence' that they are our loved ones and still alive.

For me the missing link is accepting that each one of us is Spirit, that Spirit is eternal, and most importantly that consciousness belongs to Spirit.

In 2008, Avicenna also showed the way to accepting this truth when he said

> *"Now the knowledge that you need to learn is brought in, it is not the thought but the heart that is required to open your breath."*

PART 7

WHERE MY HOME IS

In November 2004, at a development circle at the College of Psychic Studies with Jean Blackabee, I received a message that was channelled through me. As English is not my mother tongue, I have always been shy of channelling or trance mediumship. This was one of the rare occasions on which I was brave enough to allow it come through.

Some of you called them 'fathers'

They put their faith in them

There is no religion in our world

You are part of us

The world is full of people looking for a faith

They do not know that, they give their power to outsiders

There is no religion in our world

> *You are part of us*
>
> *We are you*
>
> *You are us*

In relative terms, I was introduced to Spiritualism recently. Spiritualism is a recognised religion in the UK. While I, personally, have never felt the need to belong to any religion, the philosophy of Spiritualism is close to my heart.

All the religions in the world have their Holy Book — whether it is the Bible, the Koran, the Vedas, the Gur Granth Sahib, etc. They all tell you how you should lead your life. Spiritualism does not have a book because it states that your life is your own responsibility. This, to me, is not only extremely challenging but in addition *empowering*. It frees us from a life based on a belief that we have no choices in our lives — in other words that we are born to families/societies/countries, we grow up, and we die.

On my return from Hong Kong, I could not decide where my home is. I was unable to find good enough reasons to make the choice between Istanbul—where my family home was — and London — where I had my flat and had spent a very large part of my adult life. At the time, I decided that it would be wise to wait and see where my next job offer would come from. Instead, I started this most amazing journey I never planned!

This book is the story of that journey.

I still live in London, now travelling mostly for my work with the Spirit or for holidays. In my early days, before demonstrations or services, I would sit quietly for a short while to meditate. If I felt any unease, or nervousness for any reason, I would hear, whispered into my ear, the words

> *"Open your heart and just feel at home."*

Since 2005, I have been given this message before every demonstration or church service. I finally know where my home is.

Printed in the United States
By Bookmasters